Britain in Focus

United Kingdom?
Untied Kingdom?

The story of Devolution

compiled and edited
by
Richard Musman

Pupil's Book

Ferdinand Schöningh

Unterrichtsmaterialien für die Sekundarstufe II

America in Focus
Britain in Focus

herausgegeben von Dr. Peter H. Stoldt

United Kingdom? Untied Kingdom?

The story of Devolution.

Texte zusammengestellt und bearbeitet von:
Richard Musman, M.A.

Aufbereitung von:
Richard Musman, M.A.
Dr. Peter H. Stoldt

Verlagsredaktion:
Ernest Pasakarnis, B.A.
Gerald Williams, M.A.

Printed in Germany
Herstellung: Ferdinand Schöningh, Paderborn

ISBN 3-506-41035-0

Contents

Words marked with • in the text are defined in the Vocabulary.

YOUR FUTURE
–YOU DECIDE
YES
FOR A STRONGER SCOTLAND
LABOUR MOVEMENT
CAMPA

Foreword

Will the United Kingdom break up?

The United Kingdom of Great Britain consists of four separate countries – England, Wales, Scotland and Northern Ireland – which are governed by a central Parliament in London. Each country, except England, now has a strong national movement which objects to the centralised government at Westminster. The extremists have always wanted to break away from the U.K. Now many moderates are also beginning to think that independence from England might be a good thing. Justly or unjustly, England has become the villain of the piece for many Scots, Welsh and Irish.

The British Labour Government has taken notice of these demands for self-government. In the case of Scotland and Wales a new word for self-government is now being used – the word 'devolution'. It is related to 'evolution' and 'revolution', but is quite different from both.

'Devolution' means 'power and authority taken from the central government and given to regional governments'. It does not mean 'independence' or 'separation'.

In 1977 the Government introduced a Devolution Bill for Scotland and Wales. It failed. It was then decided to introduce two separate Bills, one for Scotland, the other for Wales and these two Devolution Bills were passed by Parliament in the summer of 1978. The two Bills were very little different from the Bill which failed in 1977. Scotland and Wales were to have their own *Assemblies (Parliaments) with a limited amount of independence and were to continue to send MPs to the Parliament at Westminster. But in the 1978 Bills there were two important additions:

1) A •Referendum was held early in 1979 in both Scotland and Wales to find out if the Scots and the Welsh really wanted Assemblies of their own.**

2) A simple majority in each Referendum would not be enough. Those in favour of a Scottish Assembly or a Welsh Assembly must represent 40% of the whole • electorate – not just a majority of those who actually voted. Only if 40% of the electorate voted 'yes' would the 1978 Devolution Bills come into force. It was the anti-devolutionist MPs who insisted on the 40%.

As for Northern Ireland, no decisions can be made, or Bills passed, until the violence comes to an end.

The purpose of this book is to relate the history, cultural differences, motivation and problems of the Scots, the Welsh and the Irish – and, of course, the English – and to show how nationalism has forced governments, both past and present, to make far-reaching and often unwelcome decisions.

It is a book which has no ending. The ending, if it ever comes, may delight, astonish, •infuriate, •dismay millions of different people all over the world. It may be the last dramatic act of what began three hundred years ago as the British Empire. The United Kingdom itself may break up. This is what many Scots and some Welsh desire with all their hearts, and what other Scots and

Welshmen and most Englishmen •dread.
In the meantime, the new Assemblies will not give either Scotland or Wales independence. The Scots will not even get what they particularly wanted – the right to raise their own taxes. The Government at Westminster will still be all-powerful. And the violence in Northern Ireland still continues …

* For the powers which the Assemblies will have, see V.B. 3, p. 108.
** See Postscript p. 125.

Vocabulary

referendum	[ˌrefəˈrendəm]	a general vote by all qualified voters on a single political question, e.g. Shall Scotland have independence?
electorate	[iˈlektərit]	all those people who have a right to vote
infuriate	[inˈfjuərieit]	make very angry
dismay	[disˈmei]	make very anxious
dread	[dred]	have a great fear of

Exercises

1. What does Devolution mean? How is it different from evolution and revolution?
2. Explain the importance of the referendum in the Devolution Bills for Scotland and for Wales.
3. Why is the 40% so important to the anti-devolutionist MPs?

Notes on the History of the British Isles

ENGLAND, SCOTLAND and WALES

55 B.C.	Romans under Julius Caesar invade Britain.
410 A.D.	Romans leave Britain.
450–600	Angles and Saxons invade and conquer Britain. Britons flee to Wales and Cornwall, where they are safe for a while. They also invade and settle in Scottish Lowlands.
793–978	Danes (Vikings) invade Britain. Press northwards up east coast of Scotland.
1066	Normans under William the Conqueror invade and conquer the English at the Battle of Hastings.
1285	After 200 years of bitter fighting Welsh lose independence.
1200	English try to conquer Scotland, but fail.
1314	Battle of Bannockburn: Scots under Robert the Bruce defeat the English. From then on, Scotland completely independent.
1415	Death of Owen Glendower, last champion of the Welsh against the English.
1535	Act of Union between England and Wales
1587	Execution of Mary Queen of Scots.
1603	Elizabeth I of England dies childless. James VI of Scotland becomes James I of England.
1620	Pilgrim Fathers: 102 English Puritans set sail for America in search of religious freedom.
1688	James II overthrown and flies to France. William and Mary of Orange invited to be joint King and Queen. Parliament decides that England will never again be ruled by a Catholic.
1707	Act of Union between Scotland and England. England, Scotland and Wales become Great Britain.
1745	Bonnie Prince Charlie tries, with the help of the Scottish Highlanders, to win back crown of Britain for the Stuarts. Charles is defeated at Battle of Culloden. English general, Duke of Cumberland, takes a terrible revenge on Highlanders.
1750	Clearances begin in Scottish Highlands. Crofters emigrate to England, and to North America.
1830–1890	Emigration from Britain to Australia, New Zealand, Canada, South Africa and also to USA
1900–1914	Many Welshmen emigrate to USA from mining valleys of South Wales.
1926	Plaid Cymru (Welsh Nationalist Party) founded
1928	Scottish National Party (SNP) founded
1966	Gwynfor Evans, leader of Welsh Nationalists, wins first seat for Plaid Cymru at Westminster.

1969	Margot Macdonald wins first seat for SNP in a by-election.
1970	SNP wins first seat in a General Election, but Margot Macdonald loses her seat.
1974 (Feb.)	SNP wins 7 seats at General Election (Labour victory by tiny majority).
1974 (Oct.)	SNP win 11 seats at General Election (Labour win again by very small majority).
1977	Devolution Bill (separate Assemblies for Scotland and Wales) introduced into Parliament by Labour Government – without success
1978	Two Devolution Bills passed, one for Scotland and one for Wales
1979 (Mar.)	Referendum in Scotland and Wales.

IRELAND

1169	Beginning of the Anglo-Norman invasion; from now on fierce and frequent rebellions
	Early Seventeenth Century: English and Scottish Protestants settled by King James I among Catholics of Northern Ireland
1641	Great Irish Rebellion
1649	Cromwell crushes the Rebellion. Massacre of Catholics by his Protestant soldiers; further Protestant settlers sent to Northern Ireland
1688	Irish rebel again.
1690	Rebellion crushed by William III at the Battle of the Boyne.
1800	Act of Union with Great Britain
1846	The Great Hunger – Potato famine: 1 million die. Before end of century $1^1/_2$ million Irish emigrate to USA and colonies. About 1 million emigrate to Great Britain.
1886	William Gladstone, the great Liberal statesman, introduces his first Home Rule Bill for Ireland. It fails because not all Liberals would vote with him.
1893	Gladstone introduces second Home Rule Bill, but thrown out by House of Lords
1914	First World War: fierce 'British' patriotism of Northern Irish; 200000 Southern Irish also volunteered (partly because soldiers were better fed than civilians at home).
1916	Battle of the Somme: appalling losses and heroism of Northern Irish (Southern Irish fought with equal heroism)
	Uprising of Republican Irish in Dublin: crushed by British, with cruel reprisals but no mutinies by Southern Irish fighting on Western Front.
1918	At General Election (for Great Britain and Ireland), the left-wing Republican candidates win a complete victory over moderate nationalists. They refuse to sit in Parliament in Westminster, and set up their own Government in Dublin instead.

1920	Fierce fighting between British and Republican Irish – who now begin to call themselves 'Irish Republican Army' (IRA). Great cruelty on both sides.
1921	Lloyd George's plan for a united Ireland wrecked by Northern Irish, who threaten to fight unless allowed to remain British
1922	Independent Irish Free State (later called 'Eire') set up; Northern Ireland (Ulster) chooses to remain part of Britain. Britain now officially known as United Kingdom of Great Britain and Northern Ireland.
1923	Civil war between official Irish Government and the 'breakaway' section of the IRA; IRA finally defeated
1939–1945	Second World War: Eire remains strictly neutral throughout war, though some tens of thousands of Irishmen volunteer to fight for Britain. Some also fight for the Germans.
1949	Eire leaves Commonwealth.
1968	Civil Rights Movement in Ulster: moderate Catholics supported by moderate Protestants demand equal citizenship for all.
1969	Serious fighting breaks out between Catholics and Protestants in Belfast and Londonderry. Much damage, many people hurt and and a few deaths (mostly Catholics). British troops sent to keep order.
1970	Ulster Catholics accept help from IRA.
1972	Direct rule from Westminster: Ulster Parliament (Stormont) suspended
1974	Attempt to form 'all-party' Parliament smashed by general strike of Protestant workers (inspired by Protestant extremists). Direct rule from Westminster reintroduced
1976	Women's Peace Movement is founded. Another effort by British Government to find a form of government acceptable to all in Ulster fails because Protestant Loyalists still refuse to share power with Catholic minority. British ambassador in Dublin assassinated by IRA

I. What is Nationalism?

A. Nationalism as a World Problem

1. What Nationalism means

a) The word 'Nationalism'

The word "nationalism" has meant so many different things. In early nineteenth century Europe nationalism meant the •claim of •subject peoples such as the Poles and Czechs to govern themselves and to speak their own languages in their own schools and offices. It meant the right of Greeks to be free of Turkish dominance, and Italians to •rid themselves of foreign tyrants. In the twentieth century, African nationalism was entirely respectable for the same reasons.

But for most people in Britain in recent years nationalism has had a bad taste because it reminded them of authoritarian government, and with nasty claims to racial and cultural superiority.

John P. Mackintosh, former Scottish Labour MP,
and Professor of Politics at Edinburgh University (died 1978)
From the New Statesman, Sept. 27th 1974

b) Different forms of Nationalism

Nationalism can be anti-imperialist – violent and bloody as in the colonial war between France and Algeria, or relatively peaceful as in Gandhi's non-violent struggle with the British. Whether bad self-government is preferable to good government by centralised rule is a matter of opinion, but there are people in all democracies who consider this form of nationalism •justifiable, even when it is violent.

There is another form of nationalism, the nationalism of groups of peoples within big nations who wish to govern themselves and retain their individuality. This form of nationalism is particularly common today, when the world is dominated by super-powers or by the union of smaller powers, such as the E.E.C.

These groups, or minorities, are usually cut off from the rest of the country by natural barriers, such as mountains, deserts, great rivers or seas and this, more than anything, has helped them to keep their separate identity. They often have their own language and literature, their own traditions, their own racial characteristics, and they are becoming increasingly •restless and conscious of their •nationhood, resenting being ruled from capital cities which do not seem interested in them and which neglect their special needs.

c) Governments and national minorities

Broadly speaking, there are only two main forms of government: centralised government, as in France, Spain, Greece, Zambia, China, New Zealand; and federal government, as in West Germany, Switzerland, Brazil, Nigeria, Yugoslavia, the U.S.S.R., the U.S.A. and Canada. In theory federal government should satisfy national minorities, because the system allows each state considerable independence to govern its own affairs. Switzerland, for example, has four national languages, and its 22 cantons, often separated from one another by mountain barriers, get on reasonably well together. So do the states of the Federal Republic of Germany, the U.S.A. and the U.S.S.R.
On the other hand, some of the worst explosions of minority nationalism have taken place in countries with the federal system – the Biafran war in Nigeria, the war between West Pakistan and East Pakistan (now Bangladesh). The

French Canadians of Quebec are bitterly opposed to the English Canadians and threaten to break away. The Croats of Jugoslavia have already carried out terrorist acts, and the country may break up after the death of Tito.

Federal States sometimes have special minority problems. The black minority of the U.S.A. has spread across every state in the Union. In the 60s and early 70s Black Power demanded, and fought for, a separate black state within the Union, and though they failed, they helped to hasten integration, especially in the Southern States.

It is easier to understand the problems of states with centralised governments, like Spain and France. In both these countries there are minority groups with separate languages and cultures, and most of them are now demanding freedom, or protesting against neglect. The Basques, who are a completely different people to the Spaniards and whose origin remains a mystery, are fighting for independence. They have fought the police, thrown bombs into public buildings and even attacked and killed ministers in Madrid. The Catalans have also demanded a form of self-government. They have their own language and literature and feel themselves to be different. Catalonia is the most industrialised region of Spain and the Catalans have, therefore, greater •bargaining power than the Basques. They have, in fact, already been granted a certain amount of home rule.

The Basques and Catalans on the French side of the Pyrenees have no wish to break away from France. But the French have other minority problems. In Provence, some people feel there is a historical and cultural gulf between themselves and the French. Some Provençal patriots want to •revive the ancient Provençal language, which some of the older generation still speak. Some fanatics even paint on walls and rocks, "Go home Parisians!" "Go home Frenchmen!" There is no separatist movement among the German-speaking Alsatians in France, probably because they have changed hands so many times in their history, but there is nationalism in Celtic Brittany. The Breton language is still alive, although most of the younger generation do not bother to learn it. Most Bretons do not demand separation, just recognition of the fact that they have a culture and traditions of their own, but there is a small group of Breton "freedom fighters" who demand independence. In June 1978 they blew up a room in the Palace of Versailles and destroyed valuable pictures. The Corsicans, once the most patriotic of Frenchmen, now have a liberation movement which has been responsible for several deaths. Corsica is still one of the most backward parts of France, and Corsicans still have a culture and a dialect which is all their own. Their chief complaint is neglect by the central government, and they have underlinded their discontent by throwing a bomb or two.

The Azores and Madeira wish to break away from Portugal. Even the tiny population of the Faroes and Greenland wish to free themselves from the well-meaning •paternalism of the Danes. The Flemish- and French-speaking Belgians are bitterly divided by language. There are many other examples in different parts of the world where little nations within big nations are striving for recognition and control of their own affairs.

d) The United Kingdom

The United Kindom is not a federation. It is united not only by the Queen, but also by the central government at Westminster and the •civil service in London. Until the 1960s, apart from the continuous Irish "troubles", few countries were considered so united as the United Kingdom. Then things began to change. Scots and Welshmen began to criticise the English as they had never done before. Already the word "hatred" is used frequently. But by no means all Welshmen and Scots share these feelings. In other words, there is conflict within each of these countries, as well as in the United Kingdom as a whole. Why? How? When? Will the hatred ever explode into violence, as has already happened in Ireland? These are some of the questions discussed in this book.

Editor

Vocabulary

claim	[kleim]	something you ask for or demand, because you believe it belongs to you, or because you believe you have a right to it
subject (adj)	[ˈsʌbdʒekt]	a subject people is one that is ruled by a foreign power. The adjective "subject" suggests a lack of freedom.
rid themselves of		get rid of
justifiable	[ˈdʒʌstifaiəbl]	free from guilt or blame; people have no right to criticise or condemn it.
restless	[ˈrestlis]	here: discontented
nationhood	[ˈneiʃənhud]	being a nation
bargaining power	[ˈbɑːginiŋ ˈpauə*]	being in a strong position to demand something you want
revive	[riˈvaiv]	bring to life again; make live again
paternalism	[pəˈtəːnlizəm]	here: treating a subject people as a kind but autocratic father treats his children. Suggests the attitude: "I know what is good for you better than you know yourselves".
civil service	[ˈsivl ˈsəːvis]	the permanent "servants", or officers of the State who run the different departments. The members of the Civil Service are called "civil servants".

2. The United Kingdom – population figures

Between the census of 1961 and that of 1971 England's population increased by nearly $2^{1}/_{2}$ million, Northern Ireland's by 100000, Wales's by 80000 and Scotland's by only 50000 (see p. 29). The Channel Islands and the Isle of Man have a large measure of self-rule. They are even responsible for their own income tax, which is much lower that that of the rest of the United Kingdom.

POPULATION OF THE UNITED KINGDOM (1971 census)	
England	45870000
Scotland	5228000
Wales	2724000
Northern Ireland	1525000
The Channel Islands (Jersey and Guernsey)	125000
Isle of Man	50000
United Kingdom	55522000

3. Why so much nationalism? A letter from a Welshman

... There is just one big •gulf of misunderstanding between the Scots, the Welsh, the Irish and the English. If one examines the facts they speak for themselves – British democracy is non-representational. British democracy makes no allowance for any form of federal government in the provinces, although they could deal with their problems far more successfully if they had this added freedom. I do not mean by the "provinces" only Scotland and Wales. I would include Yorkshire and Lancashire, the Midlands, the West Country and East Anglia.

I have a theory. I increasingly ask myself if the dull resignation of the average Briton, his lack of enthusiasm and the apparent absence of loyalty is not due to a feeling that he is being governed without sympathy and understanding. Neglect by a government that is too far away to notice things! Where there is a strong local and unique culture, then it's only natural for it to want to govern itself ... and not have decisions made over its head about water supply, oil, regional development, employment, etc. This is true of every area in Britain. But Scotland and Wales have a special cultural background to lend weight to their arguments.

G. Williams, January 1977 (extract from a letter)

These feelings are expressed by several of the •contributors to this book. It is not only the Scots, the Welsh and the Irish who are dissatisfied, frustrated and critical of the state of British society. Englishmen from north, south, east and west are just as •dispirited. The lack of faith in Parliament and in politicians of all the established parties is wide-spread throughout the country. That is one reason why so many Welsh and Scots are attracted to their Nationalist parties. In Scotland, the Scottish National Party (SNP) has become a powerful influence in British politics (see p. 41). In Wales, Plaid Cymru (the Party of Wales) is less powerful, but has attracted many followers (see p. 64). These parties have become more and more experienced in the game of politics, and they also have ideals and enthusiasm. Their leaders are •dynamic, and they offer their supporters something to fight for. It is the misfortune of the English that they can only express their frustration by emigrating. Many of them are doing this.

Vocabulary

gulf	[gʌlf]	here: enormous gap, space
contributors	[kən'tribjutəz]	here: writers who have written articles, chapters, etc. for a book
dispirited	[di'spiritid]	having lost all enthusiams and keenness
dynamic	[dai'næmik]	having many new ideas and putting them quickly into practice

B. Big Question-marks about Devolution

1. The Dangers of Devolution

But not all Englishmen wish to emigrate. Not all Scots and Welshmen express their frustration by joining the nationalist parties. Englishmen do not want to see the United Kingdom break up, and at the moment a large majority of Welshmen and also a majority of Scotsmen are still against separatism. But in England there is a lack of interest in Devolution among ordinary people, and some do not even know what the word means. This could mean that the •delicate matter of Devolution may not be treated with the great thought and care which is essential if the United Kingdom is to remain "united".
Here is an extract from a leading article in a important English newspaper:

"Devolution ... remains a worrying and dangerous issue, boring to 48 million Englishmen and of extreme interest to 5 million Scots. We fear that Scottish devolutionary •fervour may easily •wreck the United Kingdom, which for all its faults has been among the most •fruitful alliances in history. Yet it would be foolish to •pretend this fervour will disappear. The Glasgow Herald last week published an opinion poll showing that the Nationalists have increased their popularity since they took a hard line on independence at their conference ..."

from the Observer, June 1977

Vocabulary

delicate	['delikit]	easily broken or damaged
arouse	[ə'rauz]	awaken
fervour	['fəːvə]	great enthusiasm
wreck	[rek]	destroy, break up
fruitful	['fruːtfu|l]	here: which has had excellent results
pretend	[pri'tend]	here: give the impression

2. What must the Scots do to get self-government?

At their Conference in May, 1977, the SNP made it quite clear that they are now fighting for the complete independence of Scotland. Previously they had •claimed that they did not want separation. A recent poll had warned them that only 45% of their supporters wanted to break away from the United Kingdom, and that the percentage in Scotland as a whole was very much smaller. The Observer article above suggests that the SNP are now very much more confident of winning a majority of the Scottish seats in the House of Commons. If at the next General Election they won 36 out of the 71 Scottish seats, they would then have the right to form a separate Scottish Assembly. There would, however, have to be a •referendum to see if the Scots wanted independence. This is an ancient constitutional right of the Scottish people, and has nothing to do with the passing of Devolution Bills.

Editor

The SNP ask:

> How Do We Get Self-Government?
>
> As the prospect of self-government draws closer, more and more people want to know exactly how this will be achieved. It could happen like this: If the SNP gets a majority of the seats at a General Election, this will give us an unquestionable right to self-government. The Westminster government will then have to give in to the wishes of the Scottish people. The Scottish Nationalist MPs will invite all other MPs, whatever their party, to join in the negotiations for a Scottish Parliament. When the principal negotiations have been completed and a constitution for a Scottish Assembly has been drawn up, the Scottish people will be given the opportunity of voting on it in a referendum.

Vocabulary

claim	[kleim]	here: to declare
referendum	[ˌrefəˈrendəm]	a general vote by all qualified voters on a particular political question

3. An Englishman's opinion of the Devolution problem

An Englishman who is worried about Devolution wrote an article on the subject for the Glasgow Herald in July 1976. He said that the many Scots who were passionately opposed to Devolution had no one to lead them. They got no help from England either, because the English did not seem concerned. He is quite convinced, he says, that the majority of Scots do not want separation. He

thinks that everybody, not only the Scottish people, but everybody in the United Kingdom should have a chance of saying whether they really want it to break up.
At the end of 1978 the Scottish anti-devolutionists still had no powerful leader. The chief worry of the anti-devolutionists in the United Kingdom is about Scotland, not Wales. It is thought very unlikely that the majority of Welshmen want separation.

Editor

Vocabulary

concerned	[kənˈsəːnd]	here: interested; worried

C. The Nationalists and Royalty

1. The Scots

Will the SNP accept the Queen as head of an independent Scotland? The Nationalists have always claimed that they intended to keep an independent Scotland within the Commonwealth and to keep the Monarchy. But there are quite a few republicans who are members of the SNP. The Queen's Jubilee visit to Scotland in the summer of 1977 seems to have been a success, though some claim that her reception was cool.
In the Queen's Speech at the opening of Parliament in 1977, she referred to herself as "Queen of the United Kingdom", which annoyed many nationalist Scots intensely. N.B. In this important speech, at the opening of each Parliament, the Queen does not speak for herself, but expresses the •intentions of the Government.

Queen's call for unity divides the Nationalists

By Peter Hetherington

The Queen's intervention in the Scottish constitutional debate was bitterly criticised at the annual conference of the Scottish National Party yesterday.

Although the strong republican faction in the party strongly asserted itself, delegates narrowly rejected a call for a referendum on the monarchy if Scotland gains independence.

But even those who favoured retaining the Queen as a "limited" head of state were deeply critical of her defence of the union when she addressed Parliament earlier this month. Mr Arthur Donaldson, previous chairman of the SNP, which defending the monarchy as "the bond which unites the people of the British Isles," claimed that the Queen had been prompted to make her remarks by the Prime Minister.

"He gave her advice which was utterly stupid," he added.

Extract from the Guardian, summer 1977

It is impossible to know how many "pro-monarchy" Scots there are. There must be a great many, especially among the older generations. However, Scots now boo when the National Anthem, "God Save the Queen", is played before football matches. At rugby matches they maintain a stony silence, which is even more impressive.

Vocabulary

intentions	[inˈtenʃənz]	here: plans; bills the Government will try and pass through Parliament
faction	[ˈfækʃən]	group within a political party, usually with different views from rest of party.
asserted itself	[əˈsəːtid itˈself]	here: forced SNP delegates to listen to its views

2. The Welsh

Plaid Cymru are essentially republican. Many Welshmen boo when "God Save the Queen" is played before rugby and football matches, and sing with •fervour their own national song, "Land of our Fathers". Plaid Cymru tried to persuade the Welsh people not to take part in the Jubilee celebrations:

IN PROTEST AGAINST THE JUBILEE
AND ROYAL PROGRESS OF WALES IN JUNE
WE INVITE YOU TO PARTICIPATE IN

GWYL Y WERIN

JUNE 20th TO THE 24th

EXHIBITION, CONCERT, VIGIL, FILM, THEATRE, DANCE

S.A.E. for further information from:
The Welsh Society, Coleg Harlech, Gwynedd.

But in spite of Plaid Cymru propaganda, the Queen got an enthusiastic welcome when she visited Wales during the summer of her Jubilee year:

Wales waits for waves

By Ann Clywd

"WE WANT the Queen" bellowed the crowd outside City Hall in Cardiff yesterday. "And I want her husband," shrilled a woman nearby. After eight hours of waiting to see the royal pair, they seemed well satisfied with what they got: a wave on the way in, and a nice smile on the way out.

All 200 schools in the area had the day off. Families started walking in to the city centre early in the morning to take up their places on the royal route. On the last day of her jubilee visit to Wales, the joy shown by the crowds who turned out in their thousands in Cardiff and Caerphilly was proof enough that there is little anti-monarchy feeling in Wales.

The Guardian
June 25. 1977

Vocabulary

fervour [ˈfəːvə] very great enthusiasm

The British monarch governs through Parliament. He/she acts through Parliament and does not make any poliical decisions. The Bills passed by Parliament are brought to him/her by the Prime Minister and he/she always signs them.

D. Separate or Together?

1. Togetherness

Kenneth Griffith is a distinguished actor and broadcaster, and as his name indicates, he is also a Welshman. Like most Welshmen he is an enthusiastic rugby football fan. The British Lions to which he refers are a British Isles team and so always include Irish players from Eire as well as from Ulster. (The international Irish rugby team is also "mixed"). Kenneth Griffith takes the British Lions as a symbol of the fraternity and good will which he feels is lacking in the country as a whole.

ON SATURDAY 18 June, there will be news about the British Lions rugby tour of New Zealand (**Grandstand**, 10.30 BBC1; **International Rugby Special**, 1.2 am Radio 1 and 2). I personally will wait with that sinking feeling in my stomach until I know the result – and please God, may the Lions win! Now this is very interesting because I am a Welshman (and an increasingly positive Welshman at that) and the Lions are composed of not only predominantly Welshmen (and it is not for me to argue against those selectors who say that we play the game better than anyone else) but also Englishmen and Scotsmen and Irishmen.

The significant fact is that when we play Rugby football *together* we tend to be world beaters. Is this not relevant to an argument against blind nationalism or even devolution? Of course, we are different peoples in temperament and talents, but something hammers into my mind that we are all magically complementary. I fear that in these days of united British weakness (off the rugby field), selfish national interests have seized their – in certain cases – miserable opportunities and it could lead to the end of the Lions. If, however, devolution or nationalism is really a movement to find our full separate racial qualities, together with the concept of then co-operating and playing with and for each other, then devolution will be all for the best. Anyway, God save the British Lions!

Radio Times, Junes 1977

Vocabulary

significant (fact) [sigˈnifikənt] (fact) which has an important meaning

2. In Praise of Devolution

Some Englishmen in a pub discuss – not very seriously – what might happen if devolution came to Britain:

Homer said, "It looks as though Britain is breaking up".

"You mean devolution?" said Cartwright.

"Of course," said Homer picking up his glass of beer. "After Scotland and Wales have achieved complete independence, the rest of Britain will split up. There's nothing to hold England together except the World Cup and other international sporting events and there's a lot of evidence to suggest that Yorkshire, the Midlands and the South East would do better at cricket and football than England."

"A good argument," said Carothers, "but would those separate, self-governing states be able to manage economically? I mean, what about the black spots, the areas •of depression, a country like Cumbria or Cornishland, where unemployment is very high?"

"Each country," said Homer, "would be separately represented in the EEC and would •qualify for •reconstruction grants. France and Germany mightn't like it, but they'd have to pay up: the combined votes of the former British states would always be the dominant influence in Common Market policy."

"Eight more pints, please, Elsie!" said Stonier.

"Would these nation states have a common policy in defence, foreign policy, transport and so on?" said Marsden.

"Doubt it," said Homer. "I'm quite sure they'd want complete independence. Not a bad thing, either. Take defence. Each state would be too small to run an army or a navy or to use complicated modern weapons, and my guess is that they'd all go neutral, get out of NATO and •disband the armed forces in their area. They'd be defenceless, but does that matter in an age of super-giants? Yorkshire might be tempted to have a gunboat or two to protect its trawlers in Icelandic waters ..."

"All the countries of the British federation will be poor," said Homer. "There'll be unbelievable inflation, and unbelievable unemployment. But there'll be a back-to-the-land movement. Thousands working as hard as they can – for four hours a day – to grow enough wheat, sugar, beans, soya to feed ourselves. It can be done. We'll eat half as much as before, and we'll be much healthier. Fewer heart attacks, steadier blood pressure. And because most of us will be riding bikes rather than cars, we'll be altogether fitter."

"Will we get bikes on the National Health Service?" said Stonier.

"Why not?" said Homer. "It would be up to each state to decide. Of course not everyone will approve of this new programme and millions will be emigrating. Let 'em go! We should be an infinitely happier island if we could get our population down to thirty millions. We'd have plenty of housing, schools, hospitals and room to breathe. If we could get rid of twenty millions we's soon be •self-sufficient in all the things that matter."

"And when do you think all this will happen?" said Carothers.

"I've got great hopes for 1976," said Homer. "Don't forget it's the bicentenary of our independence from America – an important date. Just think! We might have been an •off-shore island of an English-speaking Union with its capital in New York, Boston or Washington. And, heaven forbid, we should all be speaking in American accents, and drinking whiskey (with an "e") and Coca-Cola. Tell you what, let's drink to devolution. Eight more of the same, Elsie, dear!"

Bernard Hollowood.
The Spectator, December 20th 1975

Note: "Whiskey" is the American spelling.

Vocabulary

depression (area of)	[di'preʃən]	here: area where there is high unemployment and a low standard of living
qualify	['kwɔli|fai]	here: have the right to
reconstruction grants	['riːkəns'trʌkʃən grɑːnts]	money payments to rebuild houses, etc., which are in very poor condition
disband	[dis'bænd]	break up (an army) and send the men home
self-sufficient	['selfsə'fiʃənt]	growing and making everything we need in our own fields and our own factories
off-shore island	['ɔfʃɔː*'ailənd]	island some way from the mainland

Exercises

A. Nationalism as a World Problem

1. The meaning of Nationalism p. 10
   1. What different forms can nationalism take?
   2. Explain with a few examples what the word "minority" means.
   3. Try and show how important geographical barriers are where minorities are concerned.
   4. There has always been nationalism in the Basque country. Why?
   5. The Spaniards and the United States have different problems with their minorities. In what way are they different?
   6. In which countries are the following minorities? Basques – Croatians – Eskimos – Welsh – Romansh – Catalans – Québécois – Cossacks – Corsicans. Which of them have used violence?
   7. Define "federalism"
   8. Which of the following countries has a federal government? Italy – USSR – Spain – Canada – New Zealand – Nigeria – Japan – Brazil – Sweden.
   9. Why is the United Kingdom at the moment in such an unhappy state?
2. Population figures of the United Kingdom p. 13
   1. Do you see any connection between the figures and the desire for Devolution?

3. A letter from a Welshman p.14
   1. Explain and write a few notes on the following:
      1. British democracy is non-representational
      2. Englishmen are dispirited
      3. The leaders of the SNP and Plaid Cymru are dynamic

B. Big Question-marks About Devolution

1. The dangers of Devolution p. 15
   1. What effects could the attitude of the English have on Devolution?
2. What must the Scots do to get self-government? p. 16
   1. How could the Scots get self-government without a Devolution Bill?
3. An Englishman's opinion p. 16
   1. According to the Englishman who wrote to the Glasgow Herald, the SNP has a big advantage over the anti-devolutionists. Explain in a few words why

C. The Nationalists and Royalty p. 18

1. What advantages, if any, does a monarchy have over a republic?
2. Find out what powers the monarch has in the British Constitution, and then make a few notes.
3. After reading the newspaper articles, do you feel that the Scots and the Welsh are in favour of the monarchy?

D. Separate or Together

1. Togetherness p. 20
   1. Who are the British Lions?
   2. According to Kenneth Griffith, what is the significant fact about the British Lions?
2. In Praise of Devolution p. 21
   1. Explain the following phrases:
      1. ... to be able to manage economically
      2. reconstruction grants
      3. ... disband the armed forces
      4. back-to-the-land movement
      5. Will we get bikes on the National Health Service?
      6. Self-sufficient
   2. Make a list of the points in this article that could be taken seriously.

II. Is Scotland a Nation?

A. Some Facts and Opinions

1. Scots divided among themselves

Some Scots, those who are Nationalists, call themselves Scots, but do not consider themselves to be "British" at all. Other Scots do not like being taken for English, but do not mind being called British – though in hotel registers all over the world the great majority of Scots sign themselves as "Scottish".
Now, with independence a possibility, there is growing conflict in Scotland itself between those who wish to break away from the United Kingdom and those who wish to remain British.

Statistics:

	1974	1977
Scots who want independence:	17%	18%
Scottish Nationalists who want independence:		43%

The British love to express their views and disagreements in letters to newspapers and journals. The correspondence columns have become battlegrounds for Scottish Nationalists and Scottish anti-Nationalists alike. There are many anti-Nationalists whose feelings are as strong as those of the Nationalists, but as yet they have weak leadership and no effective organisation. It is said that Labour M.P.s in Scotland never think in terms of attack. They think only of holding on desperately to what they have got.

a) The two letters below were written to the Spectator by Scottish anti-Nationalists. The Spectator is a London-based weekly whose political sympathies are more Conservative than Labour.

Mr Cameron refers to the election results of *February* 1974. He must have been disappointed by the SNP successes in the *October* election of the same year. It should be noted that Mr Hall lives only a few miles from the English border.

Scottish Nationalists

Sir: At a time when North Sea oil is only one of many reasons why people south of the Border should have a better understanding of what makes Scotsmen tick, it would be a pity if too much were read into the SNP successes. They were certainly sensational, and SNP are, of course, quick to point out that having gained more than 21 per cent of the poll they ought under a reformed electoral system to have an even higher number of seats.

But the converse of the proposition is that nearly 80 per cent of Scots did *not* vote Scottish Nationalist. And of those seats which SNP actually won it would be fair to say that all were in constituencies where the less sophisticated voters predominate, and in those where SNP came second much the same applies. It is indeed rare, throughout Scotland, to meet a well-informed person who does not realise that our economic and cultural interdependence with England makes any form of separation unthinkable. Devolution is more debatable, but quite another matter.

I say 'temporary' in a spirit of hopefulness. Because there is a further reason for this Scottish aberration. Scottish Nationalism tends to flare up when things are going badly for England. This is a question of history. The Scottish national heritage is a heritage of failure — economic, political, military — not necessarily always through their own fault. The Union of 1707 brought the Scots prosperity for the first time, and the British Empire for the first time their share of glory. The Scots found much more pride and emotional satisfaction in the Empire than did the average Englishman. We heard nothing of Scottish Nationalism during those splendid years. It only began to be a positive nuisance during the liquidation of the Empire under the Attlee government.

There are Scots who have a tendency to desert the losing side. An English immigrant tells me he is often amused at his Scottish friends' reactions during the Test matches. If England seem to be well placed, they say, "*We*'re doing pretty well." If England are in trouble, they tell him, "*You*'re not doing very well, are you?"

England are not doing very well, just at this moment.

D. H. Cameron
Spoutwells House, Scone, Perthshire

Scots and Celts

Sir: While I can share Mr Angus Maude's dislike of Scottish Nationalism I must protest against his use of the terms Scots and Celts as if they were synonymous (Notebook, March 23). He appears not to know that most Scots are not Celts but are far nearer the English in outlook and way of life than they are to the people of the Highland fringe. A Scot like myself feels more at home in an English village than in a Highland community. Indeed the attraction of the Northwest Highland country for many of us is that it presents a greater contrast to our Lowland way of life than anything we find in this island. It is of some significance that the Church of Scotland which is staunchly presbyterian is on more friendly terms with the Church of England than with the small presbyterian bodies which dominate parts of the Highlands. In fact, strictly speakng, most of us Scots are Sassenachs, i.e. not Highlanders.

John A. Hall
39 Shedden Park Road, Kelso, Roxburghshire

b) Scots first and British a bad second

The following letter written to Radio Times by an indignant Scot is concerned with much more than football:

Brutish, but not British

Not even the pleasure of Scotland's rather fortunate win over Wales could •quell my anger over the Nine o'clock News on 13 October (BBC 1). Like thousands of other Scottish football fans, I am forced to listen to the London-based media give a throughly exaggerated report whenever Scottish fans celebrate to excess. The intensive treatment of the Wembley pitch and goal posts' incident last June prevented the match itself from being fully presented. Needless to say the Scots supporters were identified as Scottish and portrayed as the modern equivalent of the forces of Attila the Hun. The news of 13 October twice made reference to damage caused by British football fans in Luxembourg. Had the damage been caused by Scottish or Welsh fans, then the guilty party would have been identified. Why conceal the nationalitiy of the •hooligans behind the "British" smokescreen? I am already resigned to having to listen to my country's team being •labelled as British during the next World Cup. They will, of course, •revert to being Scots when they are eliminated, or should some •unsavoury incident occur.

G. Porter, Coventry

Vocabulary

tick	[tik]	here: think and act in the way they do
poll	[pəul]	here: votes at general elections
converse	[ˈkɔnvəːs]	opposite
debatable	[diˈbeitəbl]	something that can be argued about
liquidation	[ˌlikwiˈdeiʃən]	breaking up
Test match		international cricket match
fringe	[frindʒ]	here: edge of the Highlands
significance	[sigˈnifikəns]	importance; suggesting something of importance
staunchly	[stɔːntʃli]	someone who is "staunch" can be trusted
Sassenachs	[ˈsæsənæks]	word used by Highlanders to describe Lowlanders and Englishmen (Anglo-Saxons)
quell	[kwel]	put an end to
exaggerated	[igˈzædʒəreit]	making things sound more serious than they really are

hooligans	[ˈhuːligənz]	teenagers who go about in gangs, smashing property and fighting. Hooligans are a serious problem at football matches
smokescreen	[ˈsməuk-skriːn]	here: the English hide the nationality of their football hooligans behind the "thick smoke" of the word "British". "Smokescreen" is a naval term. Warships used to make thick smoke from their funnels to help them escape from their enemies.
labelled	[ˈleibld]	here: being called "British"
revert	[riˈvəːt]	they will be called "Scots" again ("revert" means "to go back to")
unsavoury	[ˈʌnˈseivəri]	unpleasant, dirty

2. Scotsmen and Englishmen have always enjoyed being rude about each other

a) A 20th Century Englishman lists a few facts about Scotland

Scotland: derivation of the word: from the Scots, a tribe who sailed to Scotland from Ulster about A.D. 500. Area: 30000 square miles, much of it beautiful, some of it extremely •squalid. Population: 5288963 in 1971. Natural resources: oil, sheep, cattle, fish, timber, coal. Peculiarities: own legal and educational systems, the world's highest rate of •bowel cancer in women, the Bay City Rollers (Pop Group), sectarian football teams (i.e. Catholic and Protestant), drunkeness (seven times more men, per head of population, were admitted to hospital for alcoholism than in England in 1973), a high-fat diet and •picturesque bank notes. Politics: contains the fastest growing political party in Britain, the Scottish National Party. Eleven SNP MPs at Westminster. More likely to follow; recent polls suggest that nearly half the •electorate under 30 would vote SNP. Independence within the next ten years widely foreseen, even among non-nationalists.

from an article by Ian Jack (see p. 40) in the Sunday Times Colour Supplement, October 31st, 1976

b) Some comments from Englishmen and Scotsmen in past centuries.

•Oats: A grain, which in England is generally given to horses, but in Scotland supports the people. *(Dr. Samuel Johnson, 1709–1784, from his Dictionary of the English Language)*

Minds like ours, my dear James, must always be above national prejudices, and in all companies it gives me great pleasure to declare, that as a people the English are very little indeed inferior to the Scotch. *(Christopher North, pen name of the Scottish writer, James Wilson 1785–1854)*

A young Scotsman of your ability let loose upon the world with £300, what could he not do? It's appalling to think of; especially if he went among the English. *(James Barrie, 1860–1937, Scottish writer who settled in London)*

Vocabulary

squalid	[ˈskwɔlid]	dirty and unpleasant
bowel cancer	[ˈbauəl ˈkænsə]	*Darmkrebs*
picturesque	[ˌpiktʃəˈresk]	pretty, attractively old-fashioned
electorate	[iˈlektərit]	those people who have the right to vote
oats	[əuts]	*Hafer*

3. The Scottish National Party and Propaganda

The SNP has a highly efficient organisation and an extremely enthusiastic following of nearly one million Scots, a very large proportion of whom are young people. Their propaganda is often more lively and more original than that of the established parties.
Here the SNP makes clever use of some Conservative propaganda:

How gullible do the Tories think you are? They issued this map to show Scotland pulled apart from England by the wicked SNP.
Even the SNP couldn't – and wouldn't do this. Self-governing Scotland would be England's most dependable friend.

The SNP says:

> The SNP and You
> The Choice for Scotland
> The choice which the people of Scotland face has never been clearer. It is a choice between the centralism of the Conservative and Labour Parties, each of which believes in the concentration of economic and political power in London, or the radical and democratic alternative which the Scottish National Party offers. The SNP has a deep •commitment to democracy, to Scotland's •distinctive history and culture and to the social and economic well-being of the Scottish people. In order to further these objectives, we believe that the establishment of a Scottish Parliament is the essential first step. Without political power Scotland cannot control her own economy. Without political power the interests of the Scottish people will always be at the mercy of others. Without Political power there can be no hope of •regenerating Scottish society. When the Scottish people have this political power, it will be up to them to choose their own social and economic priorities.

Vocabulary

gullible	[ˈgʌləbl]	easily deceived
dependable	[diˈpendəbl]	can be trusted
commitment to	[kəˈmitmənt]	feeling of responsibility for
distinctive	[disˈtiŋktiv]	different in a special way
regenerate	[riˈdʒenəreit]	bring back to life
priorities	[praiˈɔritiz]	matters which should be dealt with before all others

4. The SNP lists a few facts about the Economic Consequences of the Union.

Statistics show, says the SNP, that every other country in Europe, except East Germany, has increased its population between 1961 and 1966. Even East Germany has increased its population since 1964. But Scotland's population has decreased.

a) One of the main causes of this decline in population has been emigration. Per head of population, the number of Scottish emigrants has been the highest in Europe:

Net Emigration from Scotland

(Thousands)

	Total	*To England*	*Overseas*
1962-63	34.0	21.0	13.0
1963-64	40.6	24.0	16.6
1964-65	43.0	22.0	21.0
1965-66	47.0	22.0	25.0
1966-67	45.0	16.0	29.0
1967-68	33.0	13.0	20.0

The number of Scots people emigrating is of course much greater than the net figures would suggest, since these figures represent the number of Scots emigrants *less* the number of immigrants coming into the country.

The SNP claims that England gains from this Scottish emigration. The addition to the English labour force, they say, is the equivalent of a transfer of £50 million of capital every year from Scotland to England.

b) Why do so many Scots emigrate?
Some say the cause is Scottish weather, but a much more important reason is the belief that they will find greater opportunities of getting on abroad. These opportunities are no longer so plentiful in England now. Look at the emigration chart and compare the England figures with the overseas figures from 1964 onwards.
It was belief in these opportunities that brought so many Welsh to England – and Irish. The SNP believes that independence would make Scotland more attractive to Scots and so keep them at home.
The SNP makes economic comparisons between Scotland and other small nations in Europe. Scotland has more unemployment than Switzerland, Norway and Denmark. Her economic growth is much less than any of these countries, and so is her industrial production. All this would change say the SNP, if Scotand could break free from England.

Editor

B. The Scots – An Undefeated People

1. The early history of Scotland

The Scots are a proud people. Their particular pride is that they have never been conquered by the English or, for that matter, by anyone else. The Romans dared not penetrate the wild, roadless hills beyond the Border, and at the command of the Emperor, Hadrian, they built a great stone wall, the ruins of which still stretch from Newcastle on the North Sea to Carlisle in the West. The object of the wall was to keep the Scots out of England.
Once the Romans had gone, the Anglo-Saxon invaders of Britain occupied the east coast of Scotland. These Germanic "immigrants" became Scots, but they had little contact with the wild Celts who fiercely defended their homeland in the rocky wilderness of the Highlands. There were no roads in the Highlands then. In the winter the valleys, or glens, were blocked by snow. In spring •torrents roared down the glens to the sea. The Highland "lairds", the chiefs of the different tribes, or "clans", built themselves tall grey stone castles, while their clansmen lived in primitive cottages built of stone or blocks of •peat. In those days the clansmen fought loyally for their lairds. Fighting was their chief occupation, and the Scottish Highlanders have remained one of the toughest fighting races in the world.
The Highlanders called themselves the only true Scots, and considered the Lowlanders to be hardly better than Sassenachs (see p. 26). It was a long time before Scotland became a truly united nation.
The English made •futile attempts during the Middle Ages to conquer Scotland. Their armies were almost always defeated, their worst defeat being by the Scottish King, Robert the Bruce, at Bannockburn in 1314. Bannockburn has become a place of pilgrimage for Scots ever since.

Editor

The Battle of Bannockburn

Vocabulary

torrent	[ˈtɔrənt]	stream which flows very fast, usually after rainstorm or melting snow
peat	[piːt]	*Torf*: very common in Scottish Highlands, where it is used for burning instead of coal or wood
futile	[ˈfjuːtail]	absolutely useless

2. Union with England

The beginning of the union of Scotland and England came in 1603, on the death of Elizabeth I of England. The heir to the throne was James VI of Scotland, who was a Stuart. He was the only son of Mary Stuart (known as Mary, Queen of Scots), who was a cousin of Elizabeth I. Since Elizabeth was unmarried and had no children, Mary was her nearest relative. Mary led a stormy and tragic life. She was brought up in France and was a Catholic. When she came to Scotland as queen, she was not welcomed by the Scottish nobles. After a few years, she was forced to give up the throne, and the nobles then imprisoned her. She escaped to England, begging the protection of her cousin. But Elizabeth did not trust her and had her imprisoned. After eighteen years, on the advice of her ministers, she gave the order for Mary's execution. In February 1587, Mary was •beheaded.

In 1603 James VI of Scotland became James I of England, but for the next hundred years, although they shared the same king, the two countries remained quite separate. Scotland was governed by Scottish ministers and a Scottish Assembly in Edinburgh, while England continued to be governed by her own ministers and Parliament in London.

Then, in 1707, England and Scotland were fully united – by agreement, not by force of arms. The most •fateful mistake of this Act of Union was to put an end to the Scottish Assembly and to have one so-called central government at Westminster. The Scots were eager to keep their Assembly. If they had been allowed to, there would probably be no devolution problem today.

Editor

Vocabulary

beheaded	[biˈhedid]	had her head cut off
fateful mistake	[ˈfeitful misˈteik]	mistake with serious results

3. The last conflict between the English and the Scots

In 1745 came the last conflict between the English and the Scots. It was an attempt on the part of the Stuarts to win back the throne of Britain from the Hanoverians. The hero of this romantic episode was Prince Charles, generally

known as “Bonnie Prince Charlie”. But only the Highlanders supported him. Most Lowlanders remained loyal to King George III and helped the English. Prince Charles and his Highlanders won victories and even reached the outskirts of London. But then the English, led by the Duke of Cumberland, chased the little Highland army back to Scotland and finally •crushed it at Culloden, just outside Inverness. The Prince himself escaped to France, but the Highland rebels paid a terrible price for their loyalty to him.
The Duke of Cumberland’s •vengeance was both cruel and stupid. He burnt villages and crops. He shot prisoners in cold blood and tortured and whipped men and women. He even forbade the Highlanders to wear their kilts. He earned the name of “Butcher Cumberland”, and that is what he is still called today.

Editor

Vocabulary

crushed	[krʌʃt]	destroyed completely
vengeance	[ˈvendʒəns]	cruel punishment of person who has done you harm

The Battle of Culloden

4. Tragedy in the Highlands

a) The Highland Chiefs and the Clearances

Once the Highland Chiefs lost their powers (after the Battle of Culloden) many of them also lost any •parental interest in their clansmen. During the next hundred years they continued the work of the English General Cumberland's soldiers. So that they might rent out their glens and braes (hillsides) at a good profit to sheep farmers from the Lowlands and England, they cleared the crofts, or tiny farms, of men, women and children, using police and soldiers where necessary.

from "Culloden", by John Prebble

This action on the part of the chiefs is known as "the clearances".

b) The brutality of the Clearances

Four miles down the glen the police (who were Scottish) found their road blocked by sixty women, with a dozen or so men behind them. The women had drawn their red shawls over their heads and were waiting silently.
The sheriff shouted at the women in •Gaelic and told them that they must clear the way for the law. The women did not move. The sheriff then looked over his shoulder at the police superintendents. "Clear the way," he ordered. Several of the women later said that he added: "Knock them down".
The constables went forward with their •batons lifted. Most of the men, it seems, ran away immediately, leaving the women alone. The attack by the police was short, brutal and bloody. "The police struck with all their force," said Ross (a Highland chieftain), "not only when knocking them down, but after the women were on the ground. They beat and kicked them as they lay in their own blood."
Twenty women and girls were seriously wounded and one woman of 47, the mother of seven children, was killed ... The police then went on and did their duty.

from "the Highland Clearances", by John Prebble

Their "duty" was to burn down the cottages so that they could no longer be lived in. Occasionally people who could not, or would not, leave died in the flames.
So the Highlanders, having lost their homes, emigrated by the tens of thousands to Canada, Australia, New Zealand, South Africa, the USA, and, of course, to the Lowlands of Scotland and to England.

Vocabulary

parental interest	[pəˈrentl ˈintərest]	interest of a parent in its child, or boss's interest in people who work for him

Gaelic	['geilik]	Celtic language spoken in the Highlands
baton	['bætən]	hard, heavy stick used (today only occasionally) by police at demonstrations which become violent

5. Why the English have reason to be grateful to the Scots

a) Empire days

The Scots played a major part in building the British Empire, not only as soldiers, but also as administrators, doctors, engineers, policemen, and above all as settlers in the new lands, where many of them rose to positions of honour and trust.
The English got on well with the Scots and regarded them as fellow Britons. They respected their courage, intelligence and •toughness, and they enjoyed their humour. The Scots never lost their accents, and Scottish officers never attempted to speak like the English "gentlemen" and officers with whom they worked. Nor did the English officers expect them to. The Scottish accent was a •reminder that the English and the Scots were different.
In those imperial days the Scots were proud of being British, but they were prouder still of being Scottish. Many of them considered their race superior to that of the English. During the 18th, 19th and first half of the 20th centuries, there was a full partnership between the Scots and the English. Countless thousands of Scots died willingly for the Empire, *their* Empire.

Editor

b) Great men of Scotland

Two nations took shape because of the geographical fact of the Solway Firth and the Cheviot Hills, plus the wild country on either side. Up to the time of the uniting of the Kingdoms, Scotland was much more in touch with the Continent of Europe than with England ...
When the Scots went down to England, after the mid-eighteenth century, they took something with them: the Adam brothers – architecture; the Hunter brothers – modern surgery; James Watt – the steam engine; Murdoch – coal gas; Macadam – road-making; Telford – civil engineering (bridges); Adam Smith – new outlook in economics.

from a letter from A.W. Mackintosh, Leicester, published in the Listener, March 31st, 1977.

Vocabulary

toughness	['tʌfnis]	great strength, ability to live and work in very difficult conditions
reminder	[ri'maində]	something which makes you remember
surgery	['sə:dʒəri]	here: treating illnesses and wounds by cutting open the body with the surgeon's knife

C. What the SNP Wants – and the Reason Why

1. The new appeal of Nationalism

Few people have understood the problems of nationalism better than John Mackintosh, Scottish Labour MP and Professor of Politics at Edinburgh University, who died tragically in 1978. John Mackintosh was a patriotic Scot who wanted a broad measure of self-government, but was strongly opposed to separatism. He believed that a Scotland with a fair and sensible measure of independence should remain within the United Kingdom. It was not lack of freedom which inspired the Scottish Nationalists, Professor Mackintosh wrote. "They had had the freedom of the vote for a century, so they could not argue they were being suppressed." But there were other cases of nationalism. The following extracts are taken from an article by John Mackintosh in the New Statesman, September 27th, 1974:

There was a famous Scottish poet, Hugh McDiarmid, who listed his hobby in *"Who's Who" as "Anglophobia" (hatred of the English). There were people who objected to the title "Queen Elizabeth II" because the first Queen Elizabeth had been Queen of England *before* the union of the two countries. But although many Scotsmen of the 1950s and early 1960s regarded these nationalists as slightly mad, these same people were conscious of being Scottish as well as British. Scots who go to work in the South of England feel that they are in a foreign country, and apart from the language problem they often say that they feel more at home in Oslo and Copenhagen than in London. I remember once feeling annoyed when a former editor of the New Statesman told me that all Welsh were thieves, and I was really angry when he said, quite seriously, that there could be no talent in Scotland, because anyone of ability was sure to have left to take a job in London.

John Mackintosh goes on to explain that life in Scotland is in many ways very different from life in England. The Scots have their own Church Assembly in Edinburgh, which is a kind of parliament. They have their own education system (see p. 105). There are Scottish traditions which go back to before the Act of Union in 1707.

Race and Language

Language does not •arouse national feelings among the Scots, for only some 60000 out of five million Scots speak •Gaelic. Race, too, has left no clear-cut Scottish characteristics. Scots with Celtic blood live in the north-west. The Orkney and Shetland islands were once settled by Norsemen. In the 19th century the Irish poured into the Clyde and have left their mark, and the Borders and the east coast are of Anglo-Saxon origin. But the uniting influence of common systems of education, local government, law and religion have given all those who have been to school, lived and worked in the country a sense of being Scottish.

* "Who's Who" is a book published each year with information about well-known people

The "British" Scots

At the same time, the Scots have also been British for two centuries, a fact in which they take reasonable pride. The Union brought prosperity to Scotland, and the Scots took pride in the Empire and considerably increased its population. Then there were also opportunities in England, and to be British was to be part of a great country which led the world in industrialisation, had a high standard of life and an effective form of parliamentary democracy. Then there were the Scottish regiments. It was a clever idea to recruit Highlanders, not long after the *Rebellion of 1745, in a series of regiments which were allowed to wear the kilt (forbidden to civilians) and be led by bagpipes. These regiments were entirely Scottish and yet were proud to fight in the British army and share its victories and its dangers.

The Scots fought with a fierce patriotism in the First and Second World Wars. At the beginning of the First World War they went into battle wearing their kilts and the Germans called them "the Women of Hell".

* *Rebellion of '45 see P. 32*

Why does Nationalism appeal to the Scots?

For more than two centuries after the Union there was no Scottish national party. In fact, Scottish nationalism hardly existed. The people of Scotland voted for the same political parties as the English and the Welsh: Liberal (Whig) and Conservative (Tory), and from the end of the last century onwards, Labour. At the beginning of the twentieth century, the Labour Party began to win the support of the Scots. By the mid-twentieth century, the Liberals had lost nearly all their seats, and the Conservatives no longer had such a strong appeal for the Scottish middle classes, because in Scotland the Conservative Party remained largely in the hands of aristocratic families whose sons were educated in England. This group was part of the U.K. ruling class. They had Scottish names, but they were Anglo-Scots and did not feel •at ease amongst Scotsmen.
All these examples suggest that it might be difficult to explain the present anti-English feelings and demonstrations in Scotland. John Mackintosh explains how it happened:

How the Scottish National Party became strong

The Scottish National Party became strong because a series of events in the world and in the United Kingdom made the British side of the •dual nationality less and less attractive. For the first time in 200 years, some Scots began to doubt whether this British side was worth keeping.
We all know that the British no longer have a high opinion of themselves, and that their self-confidence is growing less and less. We slid from being a world power during the war and in the post-war period became just a major European power. Then the question was, was there really a place for us in the New Europe; we sank behind France and Germany as European powers and now Chancellor Schmidt says he is too busy to waste his time on the "misery of

England and Italy". The forecastes are that Britain in the 1980s will have fallen behind till her standard of living is no higher than that of Greece or Spain. There is a sense of failure in the country, a lack of faith in both major political parties.
In Scotland there is no such problem. If you can't be proud of being British, just be Scottish. That is the advantage of dual nationality. It is an •"opt out" solution. Each person can imagine the kind of alternative to being British which he or she wants. For example, Scotland could take her place in the European Community, or she could stand proudly alone, like Norway.

According to Professor Mackintosh many Scots still feel British, and the SNP admits that an independent Scotland might have difficulty in finding good leaders, "but," he asks, "could anything Scotland did be worse than British foreign policies that have filled our friends abroad with a mixture of despair and disgust?"

There comes a moment when different individuals at different times suddenly wonder if this nationalist idea does not make some sense after all. For me that moment came at an international conference, after hearing a British minister make a statement which filled me with shame. The chairman turned to me and asked me to speak. I found myself saying almost without thinking: "I am from Scotland, and I must say that I have no part in what you have just heard". As I left, the Parisian taxi driver said: "From your accent, I can tell you're not French – where do you come from?" Again, I found myself saying, "Scotland". "Ah," he replied. "I hear it is a beautiful country with brave people; what a pity you have to cross England to get there". I could only agree.

John Mackintosh finishes his article by saying that it does not matter what the other parties say or do. It will have little effect on the Scots, as long as there is no pride in being British. The Scots will only vote with enthusiasm for a government that makes them feel Britain is a successful, worth-while country to live in.

Vocabulary

arouse	[ə'rauz]	awaken
Gaelic	['geilik]	Celtic language spoken in parts of the Highlands and Islands of Scotland
at ease	[æt i:z]	comfortable, as if they were at home
opt out		make the choice of getting out
dual nationality	['dju(:)əl ˌnæʃə'næliti]	being a citizen of two nations at the same time

2. We don't want to leave you, but we think we ought to go!

Many Scots have become Nationalists because they believe that Scotland is not getting its fair share out of the Union with England. Yet, according to the author of the text which follows, more public money is spent per head of population in Scotland than in England, and there are proportionately more Scottish M.P.s at Westminster than English.

"The trouble is, after 270 years of union," says the author, "the English know disturbingly little about the country north of the Border." (see map p. 126). And, the author might have added, it doesn't seem to occur to them that Scotland might one day leave the U.K.

"O flower of Scotland, when shall we see
Your like again?
That fought and died for
Your •wee bit hill and glen."

These are the words to a song which is well on the way to becoming a new national anthem. They are not old words, it is not an old tune – both were composed in the early seventies. It makes no mention of North Sea oil. It refers, ridiculously, to hills and glens – which the great majority of Scottish people have not lived on or in for hundreds of years – and later to Bannockburn, a feudal battle fought in 1314. Yet "Flower of Scotland" is immensely popular, sweeping across football crowds at cup finals, and sung with •vigour and much feeling.
•Puzzled anti-nationalists in Scotland explain it by comparing it with the pre-war songs of Fascist Europe. But the SNP leadership behaves in a far more civilised way than any pre-war Fascist leaders, and its supporters have not yet beaten up any English tourists. Of course there *is* anti-English feeling in Scotland – there's lots of it. Rugby and soccer crowds chant, "We hate the English" at international matches. Scottish students complain bitterly that they can't get into their own universities because they're full of "foreigners" up from the rich south.

The Scots are a sentimental people, says the author. Sentimental nationalism, to be really successful, needs an oppressor and what better oppressor than the English?

The author speaks to an old-style nationalist.

Wendy Wood, the 83-year-old leader of a group called "The Scottish Patriots", who has fasted and gone to prison for "fighting for Scotland", expresses a common complaint when she says: "Yes, I know it's wrong of me to dislike the English as a race, but I simply can't help it. It's English snobbery I can't stand." Wendy Wood has rich memories of the days when nationalism meant tearing down Union Jacks and (in the fifties after Elizabeth was crowned Queen) blowing up letter-boxes which had the Royal Arms on them. The new Queen, they objected, was Elizabeth II of England and Wales, but only Elizabeth the First of Scotland.

Anti-Natonalist Scots

But many Scots do not care about nationalism and many more are violently opposed to it, particularly in Glasgow and the depressed Lowland West, where the economic advantages of North Sea oil are less obvious than in Aberdeen.

Janey Buchan, the Strathclyde Labour councillor, thinks that Scotland as a separate nation would be unbearable. "If there was an independent Scotland, I'd go, emigrate. The possibility is depressing. I just can't believe it will happen." What worries Mrs Buchan is the "Scottish Character"', a •manic-depressive person of narrow views and tendencies towards drink and violence. Cut him off from the English influence, she says, and he might gain more power.
This means that many Scots don't trust their fellow countrymen's ability to govern: "The best argument against devolution, never mind self-government," says Jimmy Gordon, boss of Glasgow's commercial Radio Clyde, "is the state of the Glasgow Council."
The Nationalist's answer to this kind of talk is:
"Afraid to lose their English nurse
In fear of finding something worse."

A Scottish psychiatrist at a •Paisley hospital told me that the Scots were not so different from the English as they sometimes liked to think. But he did think there was one real difference: Scots tended to be shyer, more self-conscious, less able to express themselves. "There's certainly less tendency for a Scotsman to say something that's not absolutely necessary." This could have its disadvantages – "One of the commonest causes of violent behaviour is the inability to express yourself in any other way."
from an article by Ian Jack in the Sunday Times Colour Supplement, October 31st, 1976

Ian Jack grew up in Fife and Glasgow, where he started his career in journalism. Then he emigrated to England, like so many other Scots. He moved to the Sunday Times in 1970. Will independence happen in Scotland? Ian Jack replies: "I would say 'yes', because the economic argument is so strong, and because now the independence wagon is rolling, neither the Labour nor the Tory party seems able to stop it."

Vocabulary

wee	[wiː]	little (used frequently by the Scots)
vigour	[ˈvigə]	healthy strength
puzzled	[ˈpʌzld]	not able to understand (suggests surprise)
manic-depressive person	[ˈmænikdiˈpresiv ˈpəːsn]	person who is sometimes deeply depressed and unhappy, and at other times so full of the joys of life that he is not always responsible for what he does.
Paisley		industrial town 7 miles from Glasgow

3. Scotland will leave the Common Market if she wins independence

The SNP says:

> A vast majority of Scots were opposed to British entry. A majority of Scottish MPs were opposed to British entry. The SNP opposed British entry ... in the belief that, within the Common Market, not only Scotland, but the UK, would find its quality of life getting worse.
> The SNP proposes that, when we have a government in Scotland, all the necessary facts should be put before the people and that a referendum should be held on whether or not Scotland should remain within the Common Market. The SNP has already notified the EEC and the individual governments of Europe and the United Nations that a Scottish Government will not necessarily be bound by any agreements made on behalf of the people of Scotland by the British Government.

D. The Rise of the Scottish National Party

1. Who are the Scottish Nationalists?

If the Scottish National Party had not been increasingly successful at General Elections during the past ten years there would be no Devolution Bill before Parliament. The achievements of the Party are now part of history – a matter for regret or joy according to taste. But just who are the Nats? It has always been far from clear. Between the wars and through the 1950s the SNP consisted largely of culturally-minded Scots who liked to remember past glories, and who in a self-conscious literary way, favoured the ancient *Gaelic language ...
Some people believe that if ever Scotland gained her independence, the SNP would melt away as its supporters gradually returned to their original parties of Right, Left and Centre ...
The Party attracted more than 839000 votes in the general election of October 1974. At the next election the SNP is going to fight all the 71 seats in Scotland. It has already chosen more than 60 candidates. Of these, 26 are probably Left of Centre on the major issues of industry, the economy, and social affairs; 16 would be classified as Right-wing; and 16 more might be brought together as either middle of the road or traditionally nationalist.*

Is it a Party of the middle-class?

The author claims that more than 20 candidates are concerned with business, 20 are teachers or University lecturers, more than 10 are journalists or lawyers and about a dozen are nurses, farmers, engineers. So more than 50 candidates are definitely middle-class. Since at least 45% of the candidates are Left-wing, the SNP believes it can win Labour seats in Scotland.

* After the General Election in May, 1979, the Conservative Party came to power. The SNP lost 9 of their 11 seats, some by a very narrow majority. They continue to be a very active party.

The threat of an alternative "Left-wing" party waiting to take over firmly held Labour seats north of the Border could be used by the Government as an effective way to control Labour MPs who are unwilling to support its Devolution Bill. Better a Scottish Assembly in Edinburgh than no hope of a Labour majority at Westminster!

from an article by John Kerr in the Guardian, January 1977

* Gaelic, see Vocabulary p. 35

2. Statistics speak for the SNP

The following statistics show how dramatic the rise of the Scottish National Party has been. The statistics have been used in an SNP propaganda leaflet:

The SNP's aims are clear. Scottish control of Scottish affairs has remained its aim, and democratic action by the ballot box has remained its method. This perseverance has brought its reward and thus the Scottish National Party has constantly maintained progress on the road to self-government.

Table of Electoral Performance — 1929–1974

(since the founding in 1928 of the National Party of Scotland, which became the Scottish National Party in 1934)

General Election Voting in Scotland, 1929–74

Election Year	Con	Lab	Lib	SNP	Others	Percentage poll
1929	**35.6**	**41.5°**	**18.2**	**0.1**	**4.6**	**73.3**
1929	35.6	41.5*	18.2	0.1	4.6	73.3
1931	48.6	32.0*	14.1	1.0	4.3	77.4
1935	41.6	36.7	14.1	1.3	6.3	72.2
1945	36.3	47.4	9.1	1.2	6.0	68.7
1950	44.8	46.2	6.6	0.4	2.0	80.9
1951	48.6	47.9	2.8	0.3	0.5	81.2
1955	50.1	46.7	1.9	0.5	0.8	75.1
1959	47.3	46.7	4.1	0.8	1.2	78.1
1964	40.6	48.7	7.6	2.4	0.7	77.6
1966	37.7	49.9	6.8	5.0	0.7	75.9
1970	38.0	44.5	5.5	11.4	0.6	73.4
Feb. 1974	32.9	36.6	7.9	21.9	0.6	78.8

* includes ILP

Seats Won in General Elections, Scotland, 1929–74

Election Year	Con	Lib Unionist	Lab	Lib	Comm	SNP	Others
1929	22		36	14			2
1931	50	8	7	8			1
1935	37	8	24	3	1		1
1945	25	5	40		1		3
1950	26	5	37	2			1
1951	29	6	35	1			
1955	30	6	34	1			
1959	25	6	38	1			1
1964	24		43	4			
1966	20		46	5			
1970	23		44	3		1	
Feb. 1974	21		40	3		7	

Vocabulary

ballot [ˈbælət] secret voting. The ballot box is the box into which you drop your voting paper

perserverance [ˌpəːsiˈviərəns] continuous effort

At the Polling Station

3. The SNP's message to the Scottish people:

INDEPENDENCE MEANS:

1. An independent Parliament within the Commonwealth and with the Queen as Head of State.
2. A genuine and fair partnership between Scotland and England.
3. A Scottish voice in Europe and the rest of the world.
4. Power to regenerate the Scottish economy.
5. Power to get rid of poverty, deprivation and unemployment.
6. The resources necessary to improve education, health and social services.
7. The right to decide how to share the benefits from Scotland's Oil.
8. The incentive to increase still further production in agriculture and forestry and to protect our fisheries.
9. Effective means to combat inflation.
10. Real democratic control of decision-making.
11. Power to collect and spend Scotland's taxes.
12. Power to reduce taxation.

The Government's proposals for a Scottish Assembly are shamefully inadequate. They include no powers over trade and industry and make every Assembly decision subject to Westminster's veto.

Any Assembly even one with limited powers is a step on the road to independence, but no Assembly with such limited powers as those proposed in the White Paper on Devolution can survive unchanged. The SNP will seek to strengthen any Assembly so that it can do all the things listed above.

We call this independence. Could you settle for anything less?

Printed and published by SNP Publications Dept., 100 Main Street, West Calder, West Lothian.

Vocabulary

regenerate	[ri'dʒenəreit]	brink back to life, give new life to
deprivation	[ˌdepri'veiʃən]	here: loss of the ordinary comforts of life
benefits	['benifits]	advantages, rewards, profits
incentive	[in'sentiv]	encouragement, in the form of more money etc.
forestry	['fɔristri]	growing trees for wood or making paper
combat	['kəmbæt]	to fight

4. SNP Leadership

The success of the SNP depends to a large extent on the personality of its leaders. Two of the most colourful and most influential are attractive young women – Margo MacDonald and Margaret Ewing. They appeal to the Scottish electorate, not only because they are good-looking, but also because they have a fresh approach to problems and are genuinely enthusiastic. In other words they are not at all like people's image of politicians.

Margot MacDonald

Margo Queen of Scots

If ever Scotland breaks its links with England it will be in no small part through the efforts of Margo MacDonald, campaigning vice-chairman of the Scottish National Party. Margo is a housewife in her mid-thirties and her husband, Peter, runs a pub. The family – they have two daughters – lives over it. Because of her work for the party, they have shared only one holiday in the eleven years they've been married. She says Peter is prepared to put up with it, because he really thinks she's quite good. "Oh, he complains about me not being back in time to cook a meal and all the rest of it, and we have a shouting match about it. My answer always is, I need driving lessons and a separate car. But, to be honest, we just cannot afford another one. Besides, that'd be something else to fight about."

Do she and her husband fight a lot?

"No!" she said, then corrected herself. "Yeah, we do, actually. That's the way we are. We're very individual people, Peter and me. We shout a lot at each other, but we get on."

In November 1973 *Margo won a by-election and a seat in Parliament, beating her Labour opponent by 7000 votes. She lost her seat again at the next general election.

Margo not only has a strong and pleasant personality. She is also very pretty, and made a big impression when she first entered the House. Some male MPs, as a bit of fun started calling her "Yon bonnie flanks", after a line of the famous song, "On the bonnie banks of Loch Lomond", because of the shortness of her skirts, and they would hum the tune every time she rose to address the House. The English papers called her "The blonde bombshell". Even among some of her own more conservative supporters, there is a feeling that a pretty lassie in politics is not right. But during her three months as an SNP member of the House of Commons, she made it clear at once how serious her approach to her work was.

"There's something original about us, something dramatic, and Scotland needed a wee bit a' drama. On a personal level, though, I'm very bad at working out what other people think of me. I'm very, very bad at it, actually. I don't know whether that means I'm insensitive or not. It's only very recently occurred to me, for example, that some people may be jealous of me, which is bad. That's a weakness, is it not?"

Margo MacDonald joined the SNP just as the Party was beginning to grow strong again. Nationalism, she thinks, is an idea whose time has come, and the SNP, she's convinced, would have been in the position it is now, ready to take into its hands the running of Scotland, oil or no oil. "What the oil did, it gave us a safety-net. That's all. And you know, now, there's almost an embarrassment about it in Scotland. Because everybody is concerned about the English connection. I'm a Nationalist, and I believe Scotland should be independent, but at the same time I say, because of our history because of the links we have with England, the responsibility is on Scotland to share the benefit. It means a new type of Partnership."

Margo joined the SNP when she was 21. "The feeling of frustration in Scotland, that's the thing that really upset me. It was accepted unquestioningly that why people got paid more in England was because they had a higher standard of living down there. That was accepted as a reasonable answer. Scots had been •brainwashed into thinking that, somehow, the place in the sun, the good life, foreign holidays in special, wonderful places, was something you couldn't get here. There's a lot of people who want to see things done, but who politics don't appeal to. Well the idea of doing it politically seemed the natural thing to me."

Gordon Burn, Sunday Times, Colour Supplement, October 31st 1976

* Margo Macdonald was defeated again in a by-election in May 1978, and by a larger majority than in the General Election.

Vocabulary

brainwashed	[ˈbreinwɔʃt]	to "brainwash" someone is to "wash out" of their minds by clever suggestions all the ideas they once had about their country, religion, family, etc.

5. The Best of Both Worlds – an Englishman's point of view

Some Englishmen envy the Scots for having something to fight for.

If I were a Scot I think I would be a nationalist with a capital 'N' waving flags or learning to speak in rare native tongues. If I were a Scot I would have turned to support the Scottish National Party, I am pretty sure, in the hope of obtaining the best of both worlds.

The best of both worlds would consist in enjoying the advantages of small nationhood without losing the benefits of moving freely within a larger 'common market' and a wider range of common culture and language. If I seemed, as a nationalist, to be supporting separatism, I would •reassure myself that it would not be a very separate kind of separatism, indeed that the natural tendency of the Scottish and English nations – once Home Rule was established – would be to draw together and not pull apart.

One reason I would call myself a nationalist if I was a Scot would be to escape from British two-party and two-and-a-half party politics. For an Englishman there is no effective escape. The Scots are uniquely lucky in having the SNP as a reasonable alternative to the pattern of party politics which is becoming less and less popular with the rest of the British ...

If I was a Scot I would not feel obliged to justify my nationalist sympathies in terms of 'capitalist' or 'socialist'. Rather I would invest my hopes in the creative enthusiasm of becoming a nation once more, and in the joy of being set free from the dead-weight of British political life and I would hope to obtain these opportunities for my country without a quarrel or unnatural separation.

'Seeing It Scots', by Peter Jenkins,
the Guardian, January 1977

Vocabulary

reassure myself	[ˈriːəˈʃuə]	make myself realise, believe

6. Kitsch and Scottish Nationalism

Scotland is booming with more than oil. It's selling entertainment, too. Americans, Australians, even the Chinese are mad about Scotland's special kind of rough, noisy sentimentality. South of the Border the stars are hardly known. But in Scotland they grow fat and famous.

Year in, year out Scottish entertainers sell large numbers of Scottish records, not only to Scots but also to exiled Scots, in New York, Toronto, Vancouver, Sydney – all over the world. Famous Scottish regiments also make successful records. As for the manufacturers of tartan cloth, they say that home sales are now greater than sales abroad. According to the Scottish Tartan Society, the country has "tartan fever". There are times when it seems a tartan label will sell almost anything.

No matter how much pain it gives to the SNP, Scottish kitsch is definitely loaded with nationalism, and touched here and there with Anglophobia. Take, for example, "The Tartan Musketeers", a highly successful pantomime showing at the Glasgow Pavilion: on the safety curtain there was a map of Scotland in which all the towns had names like Aber*oil*, Inver*oil*, Glen*oil*, and there was a •slogan at the top, claiming "It's our oil"; the black-hearted villain of the panto was the only member of the cast with an English accent. The biggest applause went to the two singers who sang "Flower of Scotland". One of them went down on his knees and with his hand over his heart sang about the heroes who had fought and died for" ... their wee bit of glen ... Aye, Missus, *your* bit of glen."

But it may be that the ever-growing SNP and all the other forces of nationalism and separatism in Scotland owe more to Scottish kitsch, or tartanry, than they would care to admit.

from a report by George Rosie, Sunday Times Colour Supplement, October 31, 1976

Vocabulary

slogan	[ˈsləugən]	a short, clever phrase used in advertising to attract attention

E. North Sea Oil – Who Owns It?

1. What the SNP thinks

a) Scotland owns Scottish oil

> The international agreement on the •exploitation of the Continental Shelf (in the North Sea) makes it quite clear that a self-governing Scotland will automatically own and control all the oil found off the coast of Scotland ...
> Before it was realised that oil existed in Scottish waters, the British Government strengthened Scotland's right by making the Continental Shelf north of the Scottish-English Border subject to Scottish law.

Quote from BBC PANORAMA

"Scottish Oil can make an independent Scotland the most stable and prosperous country in Europe . . . or it can give temporary assistance to the U.K. balance of payments.
It can not do both !"

"Panorama" is a weekly BBC Television programme about important subjects in the world news.

b) How much is the oil worth?

The SNP says:

> With self-government Scotland's oil is worth at least £100 000 000 000, or £1 000 000 000 a year for 100 years. But if London control continues, all Scotland will gain from her oil is a few thousand jobs for a few years only, and very little else.

c) **Scotland's Oil: Where will it go?**

SCOTLAND'S OIL: WHERE WILL IT GO?

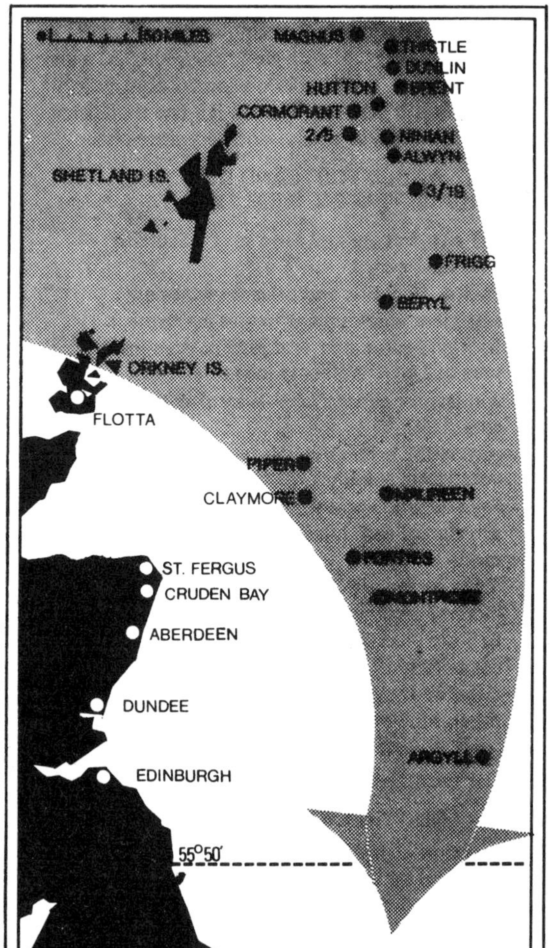

This map shows the major oil fields so far discovered. All of these are in Scottish waters.

What it doesn't show is who will get the cash benefits from Scotland's oil.

Westminster has already decided. All the cash will go straight to England—with a few pounds handed back in "subsidies" for which we shall be expected to be duly grateful.

d) What can we do to make sure Scotland benefits?

> Action is urgent. Scotland will soon be giving the oil away, and the •oil revenues will go direct to London. Unless we gain self-government we will be helpless against this savage •exploitation. Support the self-government campaign by voting SNP and by persuading everybody you know to do likewise. Work to make the SNP even more effective on Scotland's behalf.

e) What will a Scottish government do with the wealth from the oil?

> The great wealth from oil will be used by a Scottish government to make up for the economic and social injustices from which Scotland has suffered and to make Scotland one of the finest and most prosperous and most exciting countries in the world.

Vocabulary

exploitation	[ˌeksplɔiˈteiʃən]	a) here: making the fullest use of d) here: making unfair use of
cash benefits	[kæʃ ˈbenifits]	money earned
subsidies	[ˈsʌbsidz]	help from the Government
oil revenues	[ɔil ˈrevinjuz]	money earned from the oil

2. The SNP's success with North Sea Oil propaganda

Scottish oil was used by the SNP as one of its key propaganda arguments for the 1974 elections, and it undoubtedly helped them to win many votes. The Scots were led to believe that they were going to get all the oil and become rich overnight. Many Scots feel that only the oil could make economic independence possible. However, not all Scots, by any means, believe that North Sea Oil belongs entirely to Scotland. Nor do they think it should. In a poll held in June 1976, 68% of Scottish voters agreed that North Sea Oil should belong to *all* Britain and not just Scotland. They are not as greedy as they are often accused of being. In any case, the SNP has misled its followers. There are reasons, some of which are discussed in the following pages, why an independent Scotland might not get all the oil the SNP feels she deserves.

Editor

3. Does the oil in Scottish waters belong to Scotland or not? Another opinion

In 1968 the U.K. Government passed a law fixing a boundary between English and Scottish waters along a line drawn due east from Berwick on Tweed. This was necessary because Scotland and England have different systems of law. The British Government says that this dividing line has no political or economic importance at all.

The first thing to notice is that the oil does not lie in U.K., British, or Scottish waters, as is frequently claimed, but is in international waters. Who should have what oil, has been worked out by international agreement.
In 1976 the Labour Government nationalised oil and formed the British National Oil Corporation. The SNP entered with •guns blazing at everyone. The oil companies, they declared, who were quite openly profiteering, treated the Scots like "tartan coolies" and would make ten times as much profit in the North Sea as in the Middle East. This was because the companies' propaganda tactics had persuaded the "weak, inefficient" U.K. government to "sell out" Scottish interests.
North Sea oil is of extreme interest to the SNP, because it shows the people quite clearly that the country could have independence without economic loss. Propaganda leaflets proclaiming "Your choice – Poor British or Rich Scots" have had their intended effect, and the 1973 campaign "It's Scotland's Oil" was probably the most successful campaign ever carried out there. The value of oil income was translated into pounds per week for every Scot, and a section "What's In It For You?" (What will you get from it?) promised a minimum of 20000 new and 30000 modernised houses per year, large increases in •expenditure on education, and petrol at 25p per gallon.

based on an article by G. W. Lee,
the Political Quarterly, July-Sept., 1976

Vocabulary

guns blazing	[gʌnz bleiziŋ]	a lot of guns firing at the same time
expenditure	[eksˈpenditʃə]	money spent

4. Political Parties and North Sea oil

The success of the SNP in 1974 forced the other political parties to discuss the sharing of the oil wealth in more detail. The Labour Party said they were determined that oil income should benefit the whole of the U.K., but pointed out that they would be able to use part of the money for improving conditions in Scotland, particularly on Clydeside. The Conservatives said that if they were in power they intended to use the profits from oil for the whole of Scotland, not one particular region. The Liberals suggested that Scotland should control part of the oil income, and even proposed that Scotland's share should be 50%.

North Sea Oil Press Conference

Most Scots would consider the Liberal proposal fair, but •negotiable, as they have been encouraged to think of the oil as Scottish. Yet over 80% of English people believe that the income from oil should be shared equally among the whole population of the U.K. This could be the cause of conflict. The Economist, after strongly criticising the English failure to realise the dangers, continued: "The Scottish Nationalists are burying their heads in the sand, too. They are shutting their eyes to the explosive dangers of the situation. But the English will one day wake up to what is happening. An extreme claim by the SNP that the oil is theirs will without doubt produce an English •backlash." The warning should be taken seriously, because the English may not be immune to the worldwide rise in nationalism. On the other hand, Englishmen seem to imagine there would be no need for devolution without the oil. That is a serious and dangerous mistake.

The oil has come to be seen as Britain's "lifebelt", an escape from economic and psychological depression. Debts borrowed on the strength of North Sea oil could be as high as £21 billion by 1980. The SNP say that these debts are not Scotland's debts. It is not difficult to imagine what would happen if Scotland and England failed to agree about oil wealth. Terrorist activity would propably start again. People will wonder what has happened to the trust, tolerance and moderation which they have come to regard as essential parts of British political culture.

It would therefore be advisable for the Government to produce a paper stating in some detail where and how the money will be spent, beginning with Clydeside. There is not much time left.

based on an article by G. W. Lee, the Political Quarterly, July–September, 1976

Vocabulary

negotiable	[niˈgəuʃjəbl]	could be discussed, or argued about
backlash		make the English angry as a result of their extreme claim

5. A part of Scotland where Devolution is not popular

In the far north of Scotland, 130 miles from the mainland, there is a group of about 200 wind-swept islands, only twenty-four of which are inhabited. They are known as the Shetlands. The total population is 18 000, and the origin of the people is Norse, not Celtic, so they feel closer links with Norway than with Scotland. They have for many years voted a Liberal candidate into Parliament. Until the discovery of oil, the inhabitants of these lonely islands lived mainly from fishing and simple farming. A few tourists visited the islands every year, especially bird-lovers. Now the islands are crowded with oil men, for about two-thirds of all North Sea oil has been discovered in waters off the Shetlands.

The Scottish Nationalists are getting more and more disturbed by what is going on in the Shetlands. They claim that the Shetlands have always been part of Scotland, and that therefore the oil is Scottish oil. At the moment the Shetlanders' reply is that they want nothing to do with devolution and even less with an independent Scotland run by the SNP. They are afraid that an independent Scotland might upset their excellent relationship with the oil companies, who reward them generously for their services. They are determined at all costs to stay with England and the Parliament at Westminster, or else to ask for a limited independence.

If the Shetlanders get their way, an independent Scotland would find it very difficult to prove a claim to any oil in Shetland waters. The importance of Shetland oil is shown in the following extract from an article in the Guardian.

Editor

The Shetlands – lying close to the richest oilfields in the North Sea – play, after all, the most vital part in the whole North Sea oil programme, with their huge oil port, storage tanks, pipelines and stocks of supplies. And, as the Shetlanders never tire of repeating, their cooperation is vital if the programme is to keep up to time.

"We have sacrificed almost everything in the national interest – our traditional industries have been ruined – for oil, and we deserve something in return from Westminster," said a member of the Shetland Islands Council. "We are determined to •safeguard our agreements with the oil companies."

Peter Hetherington in
the Guardian, January 4th 1977

Vocabulary

safeguard	[ˈseifgɑːd]	protect, not allow anyone to interfere with

The SNP asks:

> Would remote parts such as Shetland and Orkney benefit from self-government? Are they Scottish anyway?
> If not Scottish what are they? Except for a brief spell of Viking occupation they have always been part of the territory and the political organisations out of which Scotland grew. Their relationships with the rest of Scotland are at least as close as those of Yorkshire with England.

In March 1978 a referendum in the Shetland Islands showed that the islanders were very much against being included in the Scottish Devolution Bill. They wished to remain attached to the United Kingdom, but to have the same measure of independence as the Isle of Man (see p. 13) In July 1978, however, the Shetlanders agreed to join a Scottish Assembly, provided Westminster protects their interests.

6. Would self-government turn the Scots into blue-eyed Arabs?

Part of a Television discussion between Scottish economists, 9th May, 1977

Iain Clark: The greatest strength of all lies with Shetland. I do not think that anyone would suggest that Shetland is likely to •seek its own independence, but it is certainly in a very strong position to bargain with both Westminster and Edinburgh as to which country it would favour.

MacCormick: John Drummond, as a former director of Shell UK, how do you think an independent Scottish government would be placed in relation to the big companies?

John Drummond: Until the law clearly states otherwise, the oil companies must pay royalties to the country's government from whom they got permission to operate; in this case, the UK government.

MacCormick: Robin Cook, Labour MP for Edinburgh Central, how do you see the situation?

Robin Cook: It is not going to be as easy as "Scotland 1980" suggests. Scotland a country with a population of 5 million, is going to be negotiating with a country of 50 million. The English are going to have strong bargaining power; after all, their market is the single most important one for the Scottish economy. Take the British National Oil Corporation. An enormous amount of taxpayers' money has been invested in it; nine-tenths of the money must have come from English and Welsh taxpayers. It is their right to expect something in return for it. The Scots, having taken the English and Welsh taxpayers' investment, cannot hope to run off with the assets.

The Listener

Vocabulary

seek	[si:k]	here: try and get

Exercises

A. Some Facts and Opinions

1. Scots divided among themselves p. 24
   1. What is the meaning of the following phrases in Mr Cameron's letter?
      1. "what makes Scotsmen tick" (line 4)
      2. "under a reformed electoral system" (line 11)
      3. "where the less sophisticated voters predominate" (para. 2 line 6)
      4. "Scottish nationalism tends to flare up" (para. 3 line 1)
      5. "the liquidation of the Empire" (para. 3 line 17)
      6. "during the Test Matches"
   2. What is G. Porter protesting about?
2. Facts about Scotland listed by a 20th Century Englishman p. 27
   1. Which facts would you pick out as strange – and unnecessary? What effect do they have on the reader?

3. The SNP and Propaganda p. 28
   1. Do you think the use that the SNP have made of Conservative propaganda is cleverer than the Conservative propaganda itself? Give your reasons.
   2. What, according to the SNP, are the two alternatives for Scotland?

4. The SNP lists a few facts p. 29
   1. Why do the Scottish emigration figures alarm the SNP?

B. The Scots – an Undefeated People

1. The early history of Scotland p. 31
   1. Explain, in English, the meaning of a) clan b) laird.
   2. Write a paragraph, showing what life was like for the lairds and their clans in those early days.

2. Union with England p. 32
   1. Find out what you can about the relationship between Elizabeth and Mary. Then construct a family tree.
   2. Elizabeth only had Mary executed when her ministers insisted she was the centre of a dangerous plot. Some Scottish authors have portrayed her as a Scottish heroine and Elizabeth as her cruel English enemy. What arguments can you find for and against this attitude?
   3. 1. What relationship did England and Scotland have between 1603 and 1707?
      2. What was decided in the Act of Union?
3. The last conflict between the English and the Scots p. 32
   1. How did the Duke of Cumberland earn the name "Butcher"?

4. Tragedy in the Highlands p. 34
   1. Imagine you were a reporter who witnessed the clearance described in text b) (p. 34). Tell the story in your own words and in the first person.
   2. How did the New World benefit from the Highland clearances?

5. Why the English have reason to be grateful to the Scots p. 35
   1. Complete the following sentences:
      1. The Scots played ... Empire.
      2. In those imperial days the Scots ... British.
      3. They were prouder still ... Scottish.
      4. ... considered their race ... the English.
   2. What were the professions of the following men?
      1. The Adam brothers
      2. The Hunter brothers
      3. James Watt
      4. Macadam
      5. Telford
      6. Adam Smith

C. What the SNP Wants – and the Reason Why p. 36

1. The new appeal of Nationalism
   1. What words and phrases in this passage suggest or state "hatred" , "dislike", "uneasiness"?
   2. Imagine you are that 'former editor of the New Statesman'. Tell John Mackintosh what you think of the Welsh and Scots.

2. Race and Language p. 36 and The British Scots p. 37
   1. Make a list of the different peoples which make up the population of Scotland. When did these different peoples, or races, arrive in Scotland? You may have to look elsewhere for some of this information.
   2. The Scots look after some of their own affairs. Which affairs does John Mackintosh mention?
   3. List the reasons why the Scots were proud to be British during Britain's imperial past.

3. Why does Nationalism appeal to the Scots? p. 37
   1. What fatal mistake did the Tories make in choosing their parliamentary candidates for Scotland?

4. How the Scottish National Party became strong p. 37
   1. Do your views of the British correspond with those of John Mackintosh, and with the views he says the British have of themselves? Write a short essay on the subject. If you have been to England, add your own impressions of the British of the 1970s.
   2. Do you think the Scottish Nationalists a) have good sense in wanting to leave the UK? b) are disloyal? c) are making a serious mistake economically?
   3. What do your newspapers say about modern Britain? Do they share Professor Mackintosh's views about "British foreign policies"?

5. We don't want to leave you, but we think we ought to go p. 38
   1. Turn the editorial on p. 38 into reported speech: "The editor said that ..."
   2. What is ridiculous about the song "O Flower of Scotland"?
   3. How do the Nationalists express their dislike of the English?
   4. Write an imaginery interview with Wendy Wood, using the material in the passage "An old-style nationalist", p. 39. Here are some words and phrases to help you: her age – prison – why? – dislike of the English – English snobbery – tear down Union Jacks – blow up letter-boxes – why?

6. Anti-nationalist Scots p. 39
   1. Write a letter to a friend explaining that not all Scots are Nationalists. Tell him/her about your interesting conversation with Mrs Buchan and Jimmy Gordon.
   2. Explain: "Afraid to leave their English nurse
For fear of finding something worse."
   3. The psychiatrist found one real difference between the Scots and the English. What was it? Give your answer in reported speech.

7. Scotland and the Common Market p. 41
   1. What could the EEC expect if Scotland wins independence?

D. The Rise of the Scottish National Party

1. Who are the Scottish Nationalists? p. 41
   1. Scotland has a population of 5 millions. What, then, is the most significant phrase in this passage?
   2. What kind of people are the SNP candidates?
   3. Why is it essential to the Labour Party that Labour MPs support the Devolution Bill?

2. Statistics speak for the SNP p. 42
   1. Analyse these statistics. Show how the Conservatives, Labour, Liberals and SNP have done between 1929 and 1974 (February)

3. The SNP's message to the Scots p. 44
   1. Give the meaning of the following phrases:
      1. Power to regenerate the Scottish economy.
      2. The resources necessary to improve.
      3. The incentive to increase still further production ...
      4. Effective means to combat inflation
      5. inadequate

4. SNP leadership – Margo Queen of Scots p. 45
   1. Make a résumé of this article, selecting only those passages which in your opinion help to make Margo Macdonald a successful leader.

5. The best of both worlds – an Englishman's point of view p. 47
   1. What attracts Peter Jenkins about the Scottish Nationalists?
   2. Why are the Scots luckier than the English, according to Peter Jenkins?

6. Kitsch and Scottish Nationalism p. 48
   1. Imagine that you have been to Edinburgh and seen all the nationalistic Kitsch mentioned in this article. Do you think it would appeal to you? If so, write an enthusiastic account of it for your school or college magazine. If you *don't* like it, then write a critical article.

E. North Sea Oil – Who Owns It?

1. What the SNP thinks p. 49
   Find out where the Continental Shelf is. Then translate into your own language: text a) **Scotland owns Scottish oil.** Make it seem as much as possible like a propaganda piece.
   2. In the map (p. 50) and the propaganda leaflets the SNP claims that all the oil so far discovered in the North Sea belongs to Scotland. What would a self-governing Scotland do with this oil?
   3. The SNP claims that it would be extremely unjust if the British Government kept all the oil. Make a list of the words and phrases the SNP uses to support this argument.

2. The SNP's sucess with North Sea oil propaganda p. 51
   1. What effect did this oil propaganda have on the Scots?

3. Does the oil in Scottish waters belong to Scotland or not? p. 52
   1. What is the British Government's argument as regards the ownership of the oilfields?
   2. Is the oil really in Scottish waters?
   3. Why were the SNP so indignant with the oil companies?

4. Explain the meaning of:
   1. "The SNP entered with guns blazing at everyone"
   2. "profiteering"
5. Why is the oil of such tremendous importance to the SNP in their propaganda

4. Political Parties and North Sea oil p. 52
   1. Summarize the attitude of the three major British political parties towards the oil.
   2. 1. Compare the English and Scottish attitude towards the share-out of the oil.
      2. Explain "English backlash".
   3. Failure to agree about the oil could have dangerous results. Why?

5. A part of Scotland where Devolution is not popular p. 54
   Read carefully all the information about the Shetlands given here. Then write an essay showing how vital the Shetland Islands are in the oil conflict between the British Government and the SNP. Before beginning your essay you should consult the map on p. 126. Do not include any descriptive passages, and you may assume that your readers know where the Shetland Islands are.

6. Would self-government turn the Scots into blue-eyed Arabs? p. 55
   1. What is meant by the term "blue-eyed Arabs"?
   2. What arguments do these Scottish economists use (other than Shetland) to show that it is going to be difficult for Scotland to get her oil?

III. How Nationalist Are The Welsh?

A. The Roots of Welsh Nationalism

1. The Celtic Welsh. Where did they come from?

The Welsh are •descendend from the Celtic Britons who inhabited Britain when Julius Caesar and his Roman legions first landed there in 55 B.C. Julius Caesar left the island almost immediately, but later the Romans returned and conquered most of Britain south of Hadrian's Wall (see p. 7). The Celtic Britons lived reasonably content under the Romans. Many of them accepted willingly the civilising influence of Rome. Cities were founded, among them Londinium on the site of a Celtic village called "Llyn-din", which means a •"stronghold by the marsh".

Then in the fifth century A.D. the Romans left Britain, and the Britons had to defend themselves •unaided against a much more terrifying invader. The Angles and Saxons, who had never been conquered and civilised by the Romans, swept across Britain, destroying the cities, killing, stealing, burning. They pushed the Britons, who defended themselves fiercely, further and further westward. At last the fleeing Britons joined their fellow Celts in the mountains of Wales. Others crossed the sea to what is now called Brittany. The Anglo-Saxons dared not attack the Celts in their Welsh •strongholds. By the beginning of the seventh century, the future Great Britain had roughly taken shape. The Scots in the north were still independent. The Welsh in the west were also free. The Cornish Celts held out for a while on their rocky peninsula, but were finally conquered in the eleventh century.

In the ninth and tenth centuries there were further invasions by the Danes (or Vikings), and then in 1066 came the last invasion of Britain – by William the Conqueror and his Normans. So the English have the blood of many different peoples in their veins, including Celtic blood, for the Anglo-Saxons inter-married with the Celts who stayed behind.

The Welsh went on fighting the English, and they were inspired by Christianity which had come to Wales in 200 A.D. – long before it reached England. The Celtic Welsh lost the civilising arts of the Romans, but they kept their Celtic language and their Celtic traditions.

Then in 1282 the last Welsh Prince of Wales, David III, was •captured and executed by the English King, Edward I, who conquered the whole country. The King made his son, also called Edward, the first English Prince of Wales. From that day on, it became a tradition among English monarchs to make their first son "Prince of Wales", but for centuries it has been an empty title. The Prince of Wales does not live in Wales, and only visits it on certain ceremonial occasions.

Although conquered, Welsh resistance was not over. In the early fifteenth century, the great Welsh hero, Owen Glendower, made a last attempt to fight

The First Prince of Wales
(Edward I presenting his infant son to the Welsh)

for an independent Wales. He rebelled against the English and was so successful that he actually held his own parliament in Wales. But when he died the English King took his revenge and oppressed the Welsh with cruel laws. In 1535 Wales and England were united officially.

Editor

Vocabulary

descended from	[di'sendid frɔm]	originate from: the Celtic Britons are the forefathers of the Welsh
stronghold	['strɔŋhəuld]	well protected place, easy to hold against enemy attacks
unaided	['ʌn'eidid]	without any help
captured	['kæptʃəd]	taken prisoner, caught by the enemy

2. How the Welsh got on within the Union.

The following passage is taken from "English Social History" by the historian, G. M. Trevelyan:

The Welsh-Englishman, Henry VIII, intended by his political union of the two countries to make the Welsh a part of the English people on free and equal terms. To a large extent he succeeded, because there was no exploitation of the land and its inhabitants as in Ireland, nor did religion divide the two races. The Welsh upper classes in Tudor times (16th century) adopted the English language, customs and literature. The •peasants, having no other leadership, accepted the course of events; but they continued to speak their own tongue and to sing its songs to the harp.

By the 18th century, Wales was becoming, legally, a land of great •estates; but basically it was a land of small peasant farmers. There were few big farmers, and few middle-class people of any sort. Wales was, in fact, an •equalitarian democracy of peasant farmers; and in South Wales there were miners as well.

In Stuart times (17th century) the traditional ways of these far-away peasant people were not disturbed by any emotional movement – social, national, political or religious. They were devoted to their traditional music of harp and song, and their religion consisted largely in the singing of hymns. Economically and intellectually Wales was shut off from English influence by geographical barriers. As late as 1768 an Englishman described Welsh roads as "mere rocky lanes, full of hugeous stones as big as one's horse".

Throughout the 18th century, Welsh philantropists taught their countrymen to read and understand the Bible ... Charity Schools were founded, and the only purpose of those who ran them was to save the souls of men and women, that is to say, to bring them up as Bible-reading evangelical Christians. In this they succeeded. A historian of the Charity Schools, herself a Welsh woman, has written:

"It would be difficult to exaggerate the importance and effect of the Charity School movement upon the history and character of the Welsh people. The Bible had become the Welshman's handbook. It's language was his language, its teaching dominated his social and political life. In it the emotional and intellectual interests of the peasantry found satisfaction. The political influence of the Charity School movement was no less important. Modern Welsh nationalism is the child of the literary and linguistic rebirth of the Eighteenth Century. Before the charity schools began their work, Welsh, "once the language of princes and poets", was in danger of destruction."

from "English Social History", 1942, by
G. M. Trevelyan

Vocabulary

peasants	['pezənts]	simple country people usually very poor
estate	[is'teit]	big country house surrounded by a park and farmland. Many of these estates were owned by English aristocrats.
equalitarian democracy	[i'kwolə'teəriən] [di'məkrəsi]	where there are no upper and lower classes, everyone having equal rights.

B. The Birth of the Nationalist Movement

1. Plaid Cymru

Plaid Cymru, Celtic for Party of Wales, was founded in 1925. Its aim was, and still is, self-government for Wales within the Commonwealth; they want as much independence as Australia has, in other words complete freedom. However it was – and still is (see Gwynfor Evans p. 70) – an important part of Plaid Cymru's aims to keep a close link with England. There should be no passports and there should be a common currency (money). Plaid Cymru's membership was 500 in 1930. By 1970 it had grown to 40000. Since then it has continued to grow rapidly.

Editor

2. Welsh Nationalism is Different

The Welsh still have their pride and they are, perhaps, more aware of their past and their ancient traditions than any other of the British peoples. Welsh is taught in all Welsh schools, and is still spoken every day by about 150000 people out of a population of three million. Practically all public notices are written in Welsh as well as English. In some cases signposts have been "unofficially" changed into Welsh by members of the Welsh Language Society. In fact, the •mainspring of Welsh nationalism, unlike Scottish nationalism, is the preservation of the ancient Celtic language of Wales and the ancient Celtic culture, especially songs and poetry.

Welsh-speaking Welshmen, who believe passionately that if the language dies, they will cease to be a separate people, live mainly in the country towns and in the hills and mountains. This does not mean that non-Welsh speaking people, the people of the large cities of the south, are not equally patriotic, but the mining valleys and cities of South Wales have, for generations, been strongholds of the Welsh Labour Party. The Welsh Labour Party is not a separate organisation. It is part of the British Labour Party, just as the Welsh Conservatives are not separate from the British Conservative Party.

Today, as in many other parts of Britain there is a growing •disillusionment with the Labour Party. In England at the moment voters can only show their discontent by turning to the Conservative Party*. They can vote Liberal, but that would be considered as throwing away a vote. They could vote for the parties of the extreme left or right. Very few do, although the pseudo-fascist party, the National Front, is growing fast and attracting a disturbing number of votes. There is no evidence, however, that it will ever be the English substitute for the nationalist parties of Scotland and Wales, even though it does carry Union Jacks on all its demonstrations.

In Wales more and more people are voting for Plaid Cymru, whether they are party members or not. In fact, having once regarded Plaid Cymru as a joke, the

* After a General Election in May, 1979, the Conservative Party, under Mrs Thatcher, came to power with a comfortable majority. Plaid Cymru won only 2 seats, and Gwynfor Evans lost his seat. The SNP lost 9 of their 11 seats.

The longest place-name in Britain

Welsh translated for you!

Labour and Conservative Parties now regard them as their chief opponents in Wales.

Yet it is doubtful if many non-Welsh-speaking Welshmen would go the whole way along the road to independence with Plaid Cymru. They feel that their future economically, at least, is tied up with England (though the leaders of Plaid Cymru are confident that they could cope economically). But most Welshmen do want an Assembly which would deal with Welsh affairs.*

Editor

Vocabulary

mainspring	[ˈmein-spriŋ]	the mainspring keeps a watch going; here: it is the ancient Celtic traditions which keep Welsh nationalism alive.
disillusionment	[ˌdisiˈluːʒənmənt]	disappointment because of inefficiency, promises not kept, etc.

3. The Welsh language: a handicap to Plaid Cymru?

Ironically, the ancient Celtic language, the symbol of the Nationalists, could •discourage some Welshmen from voting for Plaid Cymru. The learning of Welsh in schools is •compulsory. This is not popular in the non-Welsh-speaking parts of the industrial south. Many ambitious children would prefer to learn a foreign language instead. Nor are television programmes in Welsh very popular either, because sometimes they replace English-speaking programmes that Welsh families long to see. Only 25% of Welsh people can speak Welsh today. Most of these are probably pure Celts, but the people in the mining valleys of South Wales are more of a mixture. While tens of thousands of Welshmen emigrated to England in search of work, quite a few Englishmen came to Wales. Besides, the Welsh who live in the south were influenced by the nearness of England – although the broad •estuary of the River Severn acted as a barrier before the suspension bridge was built.

Nonetheless the immigrants soon became patriotic Welshmen. And all Welshmen, Welsh-speaking or non-Welsh-speaking, learn to sing the Welsh national anthem, "Mae hen wlad fy nhadan" (Land of my Fathers). The special occasion on which they sing it is before a match at the rugby stadium at Cardiff Arms Park. The •fervour with which they sing it is said to be worth at least two tries (two scores) to Wales. Rugby is the Welsh national game, and their national team plays for the honour of Wales. The English, who do not have the same patriotic fervour, have to produce an exceptionally good team to beat them.

There is nothing like Welsh singing anywhere in the British Isles and it is often an expression of patriotism.

Editor

* The referendum of March 1, 1979, showed this to be no longer true see p. 125

Vocabulary

discourage	[dis'kʌridʒ]	opposite of "encourage"
compulsory	[kəm'pʌlsəri]	everyone has to learn Welsh in school
estuary	['estjuəri]	wide mouth of a river, into which the sea enters at high tide
fervour	['fə:və]	very great enthusiasm

FOUR MEMBERS of the Welsh Language Society were fined between £5 and £20 each by Caernarvon magistrates at the weekend after a New Year's Day blackout of TV programmes. The three men and a woman got into a building at the 1,000ft. TV mast at Nebo, near Caernarvon, and switched off the power. The action was part of the society's campaign for a separate TV channel for Wales.

Darpar Ymgeisydd Seneddol, Plaid Cymru Etholaeth, Gorllewin Caerdydd.

Gwahoddir ceisiadau am y swydd uchod yn unol a chyfansoddiad Plaid Cymru. Dylai ceisiadau fod yn nwylo'r ysgrifennydd sydd a'i henw islaw erbyn Mehefin 30 1977.

Prospective Parliamentary Candidate, Cardiff West Constituency.

Applications are invited for the above post in accordance with the constitution of Plaid Cymru. Applications should be received by the Secretary whose name is below by June 30 1977.

Mrs Ann Marie Petty, 56 Palace Road, Llandaf, Caerdydd.

Darpar Ymgeisydd Seneddol Plaid Cymru, Etholaeth Ogwr.

Gwahoddir enwebiadau am swydd darpar Ymgeisydd Seneddol dros yr Etholaeth uchod. Dylid anfon yr enwebiadau, yn unol a rheolau Plaid Cymru, at yr Ysgrifennydd sydd a'i enw islaw erbyn Awst 31 1977.

Prospective Parliamentary Candidate, Ogmore Constituency.

Nominations are invited for the post of Parliamentary Candidate for the above Constituency. Nominations should be sent, in accordance with Plaid Cymru regulations, to the Secretary, whose name is below, by August 31 1977.

Richard Owen, 126 Llangewydd Road, Cefn Glas, Bridgend, Mid Glamorgan.

Vocabulary

fined	[faind]	made to pay money as a punishment
prospective Parliamenty candidate	[prəs'pektiv ˌpɑ.lə'mentəri 'kændidit]	candidate chosen by a Party to represent them at an Election
constituency	[kən'stitjuənsi]	district which sends an MP to Parliament
nomination	[ˌnɔmi'neiʃən]	naming of somebody for selection as a candidate

4. Nationalists, once regarded as a bit of a joke ...

The following text, by a Welshman, illustrates the attitude of many of his compatriots towards Welsh nationalism in the years before Nationalism became a serious business.

Seven years ago I came to London for the first time to the University. I had been there only two days when a short •plump girl came up to me and said: "You're Welsh, aren't you?" I admitted it. "Then you must join the *Cambrian Society," she said, in a voice that gave little hope of escape.
"Oh, yes," I said cautiously, "and what do you do?"
"Oh, we get together quite often and try to keep up the Welsh language, and we sing Welsh songs, and we wear •leeks and •daffs (daffodils) on St. David's Day, and we're going up Snowdon in the Easter vac, and Bronwen Pugh in the Metallurgy Department has a harp."
You see? I had to decide quickly – one way or the other. There can be no compromise. In London a Welshman must either be Welsh with all that goes with it or •opt out altogether. I opted in, and have spent the last six years trying to escape the claws of those Cambrians, with their leeks, harps, and trips up Snowdon.
Now I feel qualified to attempt a description of this large racial minority, with its own special habits, problems and •vices ... One universally observed characteristic is the well-known Welsh accent, heavily exaggerated ... Except for the special class who sing professionally, the Welsh are teachers. There are other interesting Welsh characteristics such as keeping up with Welsh culture. In practice this means reading the works of *Dylan Thomas, and the Cambrian sits down dutifully and tries to make sense out of something like this.

> Altarwise by owl-light in the halfway-house
> The gentleman lay graveward with his furies;
> Abaddon in the hangnail cracked from Adam ...

Some London Welshmen manage to avoid reading Thomas by claiming to have known him personally. London is full of men who have carried him home from pubs.

One of the most important duties of the Welshman in London is to keep up the language. This may not seem a very difficult task, but it is, in fact, not at all easy, since most Welshmen, as I did, learned Welsh in school as a foreign language and speak it about as fluently as they speak Latin. When English friends say to me: "Welsh, are you? Go on, then, *talk* Welsh", I say the only piece of Welsh I am absolutely confident about:

Yr wyf fi	Yr ydym ni
Yr wyt ti	Yr ydych chwi
Y mae ef	Yr maent hwy
Y mae hi	

It is the present tense of the verb "to be" and the only piece of Welsh that all Welshmen know ... Then there are the Welsh emotions, especially strongly felt at Christmas, St. David's Day, public holidays and National •Eisteddfodau. At times like these Welshmen who know I'm Welsh come up to me and say, "You'll be going home tonight, I expect."
"Home? I suppose so. My wife'll expect me for supper."
"No, no!" they say. "I mean Home. To Wales."
There is no way to be sure of avoiding the Cambrians in London; everywhere I turn it is: "Hello, **Dai bach*", and "Borrow my copy of "Under Milk Wood"." But there is one way of escape, which I suppose I shall finally have to take. I could always go back to Cardiff where you can be as English as you like, and nobody minds a bit.

Andrew Davies, "A Welshman in London"
the Listener, July 26th, 1962.

*Dylan Thomas (1914–53) famous Welsh poet, whose work is both very individual and Welsh. He died of alcoholism. Cambrian: another word for Welsh(man).
"Dai bach" is Welsh for "little David". Used as typically Welsh name like "Tommy" or "Fritz".

Vocabulary

plump	[plʌmp]	of a person; not fat, but pleasantly rounded
leek	[liːk]	*Lauch;* a national emblem, or symbol, of the Welsh
daffodil	[ˈdæfədil]	*gelbe Narzisse, Osterglocke;* also emblem of the Welsh
opt out		here: choose not to be Welsh
vices	[vaisiz]	forms of wickedness, immorality, or weakness
Eisteddfodau	[aisˈteðvɔdai]	where Welsh people meet for poetry and music competitions. "Eisteddfod" is the Welsh for "session" or "meeting"; "-au" is the plural form.

C. The Leadership of Plaid Cymru

1. The growing confidence of the Welsh Nationalists

There's no holding us now!

WHEN ONE is in the middle of a great electoral change it is not easy to realise what is happening, but a glance at electoral figures for comparable areas in Wales and Scotland will show, to the surprise of most people, how well Plaid Cymru has done in local elections in comparison with the Scottish National Party.

By Gwynfor Evans

2. Gwynfor Evans: the man himself

Gwynfor Evans is MP for Carmarthen, which he first won from Labour in 1966. He lost the seat at the following election, and then won it back in October 1974. Gwynfor Evans is leader of Plaid Cymru and is one of the personalities of the political scene.

There is a certain saintly quality about Gwynfor Evans. It is heightened by his gentle manner, his whitening hair, and shy smile. No one remembers seeing him lose his temper. He looks what he is, a mild and mannerly preacher, non-drinker and tomato grower.
But beneath this mildness there is a •toughness. As leader of Plaid Cymru he has suffered many defeats. Yet he •emerges as the one outstanding figure in Welsh politics, a necessary figure.
Although popular, there is a private man which even many of his own supporters do not know. He is unlike the usual politician. He has little personal ambition. He is modest and gentle and does not do well in political arguments on television. But in his frequent speeches he can attack fiercely on the subject of neglect of Wales. He knows its scars as if they were on his own body.

Again and again he upsets people, and perhaps moves their consciences, because he never stops talking about Wales. His love affair with the country grows deeper every year. Certain nationalists are dissatisfied with his style of leadership, his soft-spoken Sunday School niceness, his kindliness, his complete honesty. They would like somebody more aggressive, conducting the struggle for self-government with a warrior's toughness and urgency. Gwynfor Evans knows all this. He knows he irritates and recognizes his limits as a politician ... His mixture of optimism and sincerity, and his sense of history can be moving and •persuasive. He makes his followers believe, with him, that what seems impossible can be achieved. It is part of his fame that his fans and his enemies alike tend not to call him by his surname: when you say Gwynfor in Wales you mean only one man.

There is respect and affection for him in Scotland, too, and one supposes that his trips to Scotland help to meet an SNP need for a kind of cultural nationalism that it lacks.

At 63 Gwynfor Evans has been president of Plaid Cymru for 30 years. He joined, at 22, when it was an infant movement. It was only in the 1960s that it became a real political party. Gwynfor Evans was a candidate seven times before he was elected to Parliament.

One of the springs of his nationalism is the Welsh language: to him it is the root of a whole civilization. But he came from an English-speaking family in South Wales. A strange chance brought him in the end to Welsh. At grammar school he had to choose between French and Welsh, and chose Welsh because of his great dislike of the French nation. The language delighted and excited him. He began to like it even more than his other great love, cricket.

It led him to the literature and history of Wales. He studied law at the University of Aberystwyth and meanwhile became interested in nationalism. He read a book which explained how a self-governing Wales might work economically. And he believed early on that nationalism could give back to the Welsh their self-respect.

Nationalism grew alongside pacifism. In 1938 he urged Plaid Cymru to keep to non-violent methods, and the party agreed. In the war he was a •conscientious objector. He refused to fight. "I'm a pacifist first and a nationalist second."

Gwynfor Evans married in 1941 and has seven children. There is no generation gap and he talks of his children with great pride. The market-garden tomatoes provided a living, at first a thin one, and they allowed time for politics.

Gwynfor Evans has had difficult times; it has not always been easy to persuade the language nationalists to make room for the industrialized south Wales where the language is not so strong. There have been disagreements and quarrels between left-wing and right-wing nationalists, and there have been those who thought he did not take enough action against the Government, especially over the drowning of Welsh valleys to provide water for the English Midlands.

In the late 60s an Army sergeant and Welsh extremist, with a few others, began bombing public buildings and water pipelines. From prison, later, the sergeant was to write: "I was prepared to sacrifice my life and freedom for my ideals. I oppose the leaders of Plaid Cymru because they are prepared to sacrifice their

Gwynfor Evans at the House of Commons

people and heritage on the altar of respectability and pacifism."
The bombs, the painting over of English words on signposts, the trial of extremists who called themselves the Free Wales Army damaged the broad nationalist movement by making it less popular. But nothing changed Gwynfor Evans view of what the Party's role should be. "Anything other than constitutional, lawful methods would finish me and the party."
Gwynfor Evans is a •gradualist. He believes in achieving his aims carefully and not too fast. "We want the community of Wales to take its place in a Britannic •confraternity of free and equal nations as an island of hope in human society." He sees some danger in self-government coming too quickly. For him nationalism is a moral issue as well as a cultural and economic one.
The history of Wales and his firm belief that the people do not know it well enough are great concerns of his. "History is discovering what we are. How else can we know ourselves?" That is why, in 1971, he wrote, in Welsh, a history that was a bestseller.
He has the reputation of being a hard worker and a strong character. Although he is shy, he is always ready to talk, and is always welcoming, and he has a ready sense of humour, especially in private. This outwardly calm man, driven by a great passion for Wales and its language, its people and its particular magic is regarded by many as an inspiration and as a chief.

He has said recently that he wanted to retire from the presidency of Plaid Cymru, but he has been persuaded to stay on. As a party leader, historian and a sort of Welsh conscience, he is •irreplaceable.

Trevor Fishlock
The Times, October 27th, 1975

Vocabulary

toughness	[tʌfnis]	being very strong, and able to resist criticisms not only of other parties, but of his own party as well
emerge	[iˈməːdʒ]	come out
persuasive	[pəˈsweisiv]	able to persuade
conscientious objector	[kɔnʃiˈenʃəs əbˈdʒektə]	a man who refuses to fight, because he believes, even in a war, that one should not kill
gradualist	[ˈgrædʒuəlist]	someone who moves forward slowly and carefully
confraternity	[ˌkɔnfrəˈtəːniti]	a brotherhood
irreplaceable	[ˌiriˈpleisəbl]	cannot be replaced; there is no one to take his place

3. Gwynfor Evans talks about Welsh Nationalism

a) A Partnership of free and equal Nations

In the United Kingdom it is the most conservative who are most determined to keep the British state united. In their opinion unity is *centralism; self-government is separatism. The Welsh nationalists who propose that their national community should live a national life in cooperation with neighbouring nations are called narrow •chauvinists. The conservative view is that on no account may Wales be permitted to act as a nation; when she was made part of England by the Act of Union, 1535, that is for them the end of her national history. The nationalist idea of partnership in these islands, of free and equal nations in no way inferior one to the other, but closely cooperating in a Britannic confederation – this for the conservatives of all parties, is unthinkable. More than that they find it hateful; the idea often excites in them passionate emotion. The Nationalists are fascists, they cry. Emotional anti-nationalism seems to be created by the feeling that to allow Wales and Scotland independence would finally end the British imperialist and militarist dream ...
Nation and state must be clearly distinguished. Imperialism, like fascism, and all forms of totalitarianism, raises the state above the nation. In them the state swallows the nation. Even in England, not a totalitarian state, there is a degree of *centralisation which is greater than in most and perhaps all other countries. In Wales it is leading to the destruction of a nation ...

Wales has no state, and never has had one, to serve her. The destruction of her traditional culture is unavoidable if she continues to be dominated by a state structure of enormous power.

* Some would claim that Britain's form of government was less contralised than many other democracies. Local government has special powers, and Scotland has several departments (see p. 105) for which she is entirely responsible.

b) How the Welsh language was almost destroyed

By good fortune 80% of the people were still Welsh-speaking in 1800. Industrialisation led to the doubling of the population by 1850. The extraordinary fact is that 90% of this doubled population were Welsh-speaking. It was not the Industrial Revolution which anglicised Wales, but the English Revolution which followed it. Industrial growth strengthened the hold of the national tongue: it was weakened and in many parts broken by the political, social, economic and cultural •upheaval of 1850–1900 ...

The 1870 Education Act, which made education compulsory for all children, mainly in state schools, cut the Welsh language out of school life, just as Welsh could no longer be used in the law courts or in local government. For a generation Welsh was not even taught as a subject. If pupils spoke Welsh inside the school buildings they were punished. In this way, thanks to the English system, both pupils and parents came to have a low opinion of the language ...

The decline of the language was also hastened by the growth of the English daily press (and later by films, radio and television); English control of most commerce and industry; the development of rail and road communications; inter-marriage (large numbers of English people poured into industrial Wales); and above all the increasing prestige of England and Britishness, of Empire and militarism ...

In this way the world of the Welsh became an English world. English was the language of success. The fifty years between 1850 und 1900 saw the proportion of Welsh-speaking people decrease from 90% to 50%; and by today to under 25%. The language of getting on in the world is now the only language of three-quarters of the people of Wales ...

Consider how completely the Welsh nation lacks status. Not only has she no equality with neighbouring states: she has no federal parliament nor even a devolutionary parliament; nor even an assembly of any kind. Wales has no centre of responsible Welsh power which can create a channel for community energies and give a sense of purpose and direction.

c) Violence and national Freedom

If I thought violence could ever be justified, it would be to gain freedom and full nationhood for Wales, the cause in which most of my life has been spent. But even this noble cause, on which the survival of the Welsh people depends,

does not, in my view, justify violence. Violence involves people; violence is only violence when it is done to human persons ...
For intelligent young Welsh people, the system is the enemy, not Germans, Russians or Chinese. The British system no longer has any moral basis. Young Welsh people are eager to create a free society in Wales, and they are the future. When the Welsh really want freedom it will come.

from "Non-Violent Nationalism" a lecture given by Gwynfor Evans to the Fellowship of Reconciliation in 1973

Vocabulary

chauvinists	[ˈʃəuvinists]	extreme patriots
upheaval	[ʌpˈhiːvəl]	here: violent changes which took place (as a result of the Industrial Revolution)

D. The Rise of the Welsh Nationalist Party

1. Nationalists dominate at the Conference of the Welsh Labour Party

Plaid Cymru came in for some handsome if •unintentional praise at the annual conference of the Welsh Labour Party at the weekend. Although there are only three Nationalist MPs at Westminster they seemed to occupy a completely disproportionate place in the minds of some Labour delegates, including the Secretary of State for Wales (the Minister in charge of Welsh Affairs), Mr John Morris.
"Mrs Thatcher's little dogs", was how Mr Morris labelled the Nationalist MPs. "They should be thoroughly ashamed of themselves," said Mr Morris, "trying to bring down the only party (i.e. the Labour Party) that will bring devolution to Wales." The delegates jumped to their feet and applauded, forgetting the part played by Welsh Labour MPs in destroying the Scotland and Wales Bill in February (see p. 106).
The Nationalists, once ignored or treated with ridicule at Labour gatherings were clearly regarded at this conference as the main threat to Labour's future in Wales. The Tories – "a minority party in Wales since 1857" – were •dismissed by Mr Morris in a few sentences. Only with the help of their supporters from "the orchards of Kent and the dark satanic mills of Hastings" had the Conservatives managed to disappoint the desires of the Welsh electorate ...

James Lewis, the Guardian, May 30th 1977

"The dark Satanic mills" – quotation from the poet William Blake (1757–1827) adapted satirically. Hastings is a middle-class resort on the South Coast – with no factories – which always votes Conservative.
Even about an issue as important as Devolution, the two major parties cannot get together and discuss the problem without •rancour.

Vocabulary

unintentional	[ˈʌninˈtenʃənl]	here: did not aim on purpose to get this praise
disproportionate	[ˌdisprəˈpɔːʃnit]	here: very exaggerated indeed; i.e. the 3 Welsh Nationalist M.P.'s caused the Labour delegates an anxiety which was out of all proportion to their numbers
dismiss	[disˈmis]	here: said all he wanted to say about the Conservatives in a few sentences
rancour	[ˈræŋkə]	bitterness, hate

2. Views of a Welsh Conservative MP on Welsh Nationalism.

In the regions of England, devolution is all about responsibility and better democratic government, and that is why there is absolutely no enthusiasm for it at all. In Wales, devolution is about national consciousness and nationalism, and so we are now starting out on a great debate.

There are, of course, some very clever and distinguished supporters of devolution who are concerned only with the provision of more democratic government, but they are a small minority. All the fine words and fine feelings in Wales cannot take the nationalism out of devolution. For the majority it is seen as a step towards a separate Welsh state.

The author goes on to suggest that if the Nationalists win in Wales, "it will not be nationalism that has knocked the walls down; it will be the way socialism has worked in Wales this century." In the South Wales valleys, he goes on, Labour has created a machine for local government "that would make a feudal baron cry out with envy".

We have been on this road before. Lloyd George led the Cymru Fydd (Welsh for "Young Wales") to certain defeat in 1896. The cosmopolitan population of Gwent and South Wales was not prepared to be dominated by the voice of the Welsh country districts. The same forces are on the move today, as Wales wakes up to the real meaning of devolution. A recent opinion poll suggests that the majority of Welsh people do not want any further change.

Despite all the repeated nationalist claims, Wales is not rich in material resources. Welsh coalfields are the most expensive to mine in the UK; our "Welsh water" exports itself to England through its own natural channels – its rivers. The proportion of first-class agricultural land is low. But standards of living are not everything – man does not live by bread alone, and there may be some who would accept a lower standard of living if Wales could preserve its own language and culture. It is an attractive idea, but it forgets those who also think of themselves as British, and who regard the great British institutions like the Mother of Parliaments with affection and determined loyalty ...

from "The Welsh Connection", by Michael Roberts, MP, The Spectator, December 29th, 1975

An elderly woman leaves the Polling Station after casting her vote at the referendum to decide the fate of the proposed National Assembly for Wales.

Some people might regard this article as an example of how two major parties use Devolution for inter-party conflict. They might say that Mr Roberts does not want a Welsh Assembly but blames Labour for the rise of Nationalism in Wales. Experts might be able to prove that not all Welsh water "exports itself to England through its natural channels". Huge reservoirs have been built in the deep valleys of mid-Wales, and the water flows in big underground pipes to the industrial cities of the English Midlands. The drowning of Welsh valleys and the rehousing of the people has caused •resentment and anger in Wales. During the great •drought of 1976 some parts of South Wales were among the worst hit regions in Britain.

Vocabulary

resentment	[riˈzentmənt]	bitter feelings
drought	[draut]	when there is so little rain for a long period that there is not enough water in the reservoirs, rivers and wells for the needs of men and animals

3. Welsh Water

Plaid Cymru makes use of the exploitation of Welsh water for propaganda purposes – in the same way that the SNP makes use of North Sea Oil.

They're taking your water

"Turn off your taps—use less water in Wales" **by order** of H.M. (Labour) Government.

Yet Wales exports 250 million gallons of water **every day**—free of charge! AND NO BIG CUT-BACKS ARE PLANNED TO ECONOMISE ON WELSH WATER IN LIVERPOOL OR BIRMINGHAM.

Wales is not allowed to charge a penny for massive water exports and most mid-Wales reservoirs are run by the English Severn-Trent Water Authority.

THE RESULT?

- Welsh householders, business men and farmers pay water rates up to 33% higher than in the Midlands or Merseyside.
- Jobs lost in Wales—e.g. Glaxo factory chose Montrose, Scotland instead of Caernarfon (where unemployment is over 10 per cent).

NOW TO CAP IT ALL THE LABOUR GOVERNMENT IS TO SET UP ONE "NATIONAL" WATER AUTHORITY FOR ENGLAND AND WALES—TO CARRY ON EXPLOITING WELSH WATER. (SCOTLAND WILL CONTROL ITS OWN WATER—THEY'VE GOT **ELEVEN** NATIONALIST M.Ps). THE TORIES OFFER NOTHING BETTER.

What Plaid Cymru M.Ps and councillors have been fighting for—

- Welsh Water Authority to control **all** Welsh water.
- Export levy on water exported from Wales.
- Welsh Assembly to have law-making powers over water industry.

Only Plaid Cymru has consistently fought for a square deal on Welsh water; **only more Plaid Cymru M.Ps and councillors will ensure we get**

FAIR PLAY FOR WALES

PLAID CYMRU
8 Queen Street, Cardiff.

Please send me information on Plaid Cymru (membership 30p).

Name ______________________

Address ______________________

____

Vocabulary

economise	[i(i)ˈkɔnəmaiz]	save, use less money, water etc.
exploiting	[iksˈplɔitiŋ]	here: making unfair use of
levy	[ˈlevi]	(money) charge
square deal	[skwɛə* diːl]	fair deal, or treatment

E. Do the Welsh really have such a poor opinion of the English?

1. We Don't Want to be Colonies of England any More

Some Welshmen and Scotsmen have a feeling that they are still treated as colonies by the English. The writer of this passage (a Welshman) is being satirical: it is an answer to a rude attack on the Welsh by an Englishman.

I have nothing against the English people. I have taught the English language to their children for seven years. I only have an infinite pity for them, like one has for a dead railway station, or a tame lion in a tame English park.

More than 2000 years ago, when the Britons – that's us (the Welsh) – were a civilized people in these parts, the English were swineherds on the Danube. They gradually moved from the Danube and finally came to these islands, where the Scots, the Welsh and the Irish moved over to make room for them.

The real trouble started when the saints came and told the English about God, and how God loved the English, but the Englishman did not understand that God loved the Welsh, the Irish and all the others, too. He thought God loved only the English, so he took God's book and set out to conquer the world for the English God; and soon the Red Indians, the Black Indians, the West Indians, the Africans, the Egyptians, the South Sea Islanders, the Chinese, the Maoris, the Welsh, the Irish, the Scots, were all working for him. Mind you, he said it was for God and Queen Victoria; so week by week, year by year, as to all the faithful, he announced the collection (of money) and got it. Five per cent he gave to God, twenty-five per cent to Queen Victoria, the rest he kept for himself. It is all recorded in the New Bible he invented called the "Financial Times".

He also invented a proverb for all his colonial states: "honesty is the best policy". It is only lately that I discovered that this is only half the proverb. Only to his own children in their little prep schools and at Eton, Harrow and Winchester did he teach the whole proverb, which goes thus: "Honesty is the best policy unless you can get away with it (i.e. be dishonest without anyone noticing it)". And he did get away with it, until the Americans refused to put money into the collection. Today the provincial churches of the imperial English Crown have nearly all gone – one by one. Gibraltar, the Falkland Islands, Scotland, Northern Ireland and ourselves (the Welsh) are about all that are left to look after the old lion and his beloved Stock Exchange.

L. B. Griffith
The Listener, Dec. 8th 1966

Exercises

A. The Roots of Welsh Nationalism

1. The Celtic Welsh: where did they come from? p. 61
   1. How different was the Anglo-Saxon invasion from the Roman invasion of Britain?
   2. The English are a mixed race. What was the mixture by the end of the eleventh century?
   3. Who is the present Prince of Wales (1979)? What duties in Wales does he have? When he becomes King, it may be a long time before there is another Prince of Wales. Why?

2. How the Welsh got on within the Union p. 62
   1. What made it possible to have a closer union between England and Wales than between England and Ireland?
   2. In 1768 an Englishman described Welsh roads as "mere rocky lanes, full of hugeous stones as big as one's horse". a) how did this benefit Wales? b) what harm did it do?
   3. What dominated Welsh life and what good did it do?

B. The Birth of the Nationalist Movement

1. Plaid Cymru p. 64
   1. You are thinking of joining the Party. Ask a member of Plaid Cymru what the aims of his/her party are and, after reading the text, answer for him/her.

2. Welsh Nationalism is different p. 64
   1. Are there any minority languages in your country?
   2. Why, in some respects, are the English less fortunate than the Welsh or the Scots?
   3. Sum up the Welsh attitude to a completely independent Wales. Consider language, economics, loyalty to the Labour Party.

3. The Welsh language: a handicap to Plaid Cymru? p. 66
   1. Make up an argument between a Welsh-speaking Welsh student and a non-Welsh-speaking Welsh student about the importance of the Welsh language. The former says the language must be saved and all Welshmen should speak it. The latter disagrees as he/she is very keen to learn Russian at school.
   3. Rugby is the Welsh national game. What sort of game is it?

4. Nationalists, once regarded as a bit of a joke p. 68
   1. What do the following sentences suggest?
      1. "You must join the Cambrian Society," she said, in a voice that gave little hope of escape.
      2. In London a Welshman must either be Welsh with all that goes with it or opt out altogether. I opted in, and have spent the last six years trying to escape the claws of those Cambrians.

2. Now what do these phrases suggest?
   1. ... those Cambrians, with their leeks, harps, and trips up Snowdon.
   2. ...well-known Welsh accent, heavily exaggerated.
   3. ... the Cambrian sits down dutifully and tries to make sense out of this (a poem by Dylan Thomas).
   4. London is full of Welshmen who have carried him (Dylan Thomas) home from pubs.
   5. ... most Welshmen ... speak it (Welsh) about as fluently as they speak Latin.
3. Find out what you can about Dylan Thomas

C. The Leadership of Plaid Cymru

1. Gwynfor Evans: the man himself p. 70
   1. The leader of Plaid Cymru is clearly a very attractive man, and in his own way an excellent leader. He is gentle, yet tough. He never loses his temper. He is sensitive, sincere and completely honest. He has an infectious optimism. He hates violence and would never allow Plaid Cymru to use it. He is a loving father. He is a passionate Welsh patriot, yet would forbid any of his followers to break the law in order to achieve independence. He has a nice sense of humour.
      1. Find passages in the short biography of Gwynfor Evans which illustrate these qualities.
      2. Some of his own followers criticise him. Why?
      3. Write a short pen portrait of Gwynfor Evans.

2.1. Retell in your own words what Gwynfor Evans has to say about the Welsh language. p. 74
   2. How long is Gwynfor Evans prepared to wait for independence?

D. The Rise of the Welsh Nationalist Party

1. Nationalists dominate at the Conference of the Welsh Labour Party
   1. What did Mr Morris mean when he called Plaid Cymru "Mrs Thatcher's little dogs"?
   2. What is the meaning of:
      1. "the Nationalists, once ignored and treated with ridicule"?
      2. "The dark satanic mills of Hastings"?

2. Views of a Conservative MP on Welsh Nationalism p. 76
   1. What arguments does the Conservative MP use in attacking Welsh Nationalism? Answer in note form.
   2. The writer claims that Welsh water exports itself to England by means of Welsh rivers. But is that the only way that the Welsh export water to England?

3. They're taking your water p. 78
   1. What injustices do the Welsh complain of in this Plaid Cymru leaflet? Answer in the form of a short newspaper article: "I talked to a Welsh official and he told me ... etc."

6 Musman, United Kingdom? PB (41035)

E. Do the Welsh Really Have Such a Poor Opinion of the English?

1. We don't want to be colonies of England any more p. 79
   1. L. B. Griffith is not entirely serious in this article, nor entirely fair. Select phrases which you consider to be inaccurate or unfair.
   2. Was the Empire called the English Empire or the British Empire? When you have answered, say why.

Rioters in Belfast (1872)

IV. THE TRAGEDY OF IRELAND

A. The Long Fight for Freedom

1. Irish Misery

British and Irish history is one of continuous fighting, terrorism, •revenge and awful neglect. Many Irish still hate the English, although this hatred has never prevented penniless Irish families from crossing the sea to settle in Liverpool, Glasgow and London. Ireland is one of the few examples in world history where a country's population •declined – and declined dramatically – in the 19th century. The population of Ireland in 1840 was eight million. The population today (north and south combined) is still only 6 million.
There were fierce rebellions against English rule ever since the Anglo-Norman conquest of the island in 1169. Religion was always to play a vital part in Anglo-Irish relations. The Irish remained Catholic when the English under Henry VIII became Protestant. During the reign of King James I large numbers of Protestants, of whom many were Scottish Presbyterians, were settled in the northern regions of the island. It was hoped they would keep the Irish Catholics in check. But the violence between British and Irish continued. The Irish rebelled again in 1649, and the Puritan leader, Cromwell, •crushed them. They rebelled yet again in 1688, and this time it was William of Orange – King William III – who defeated them at the historic battle of the Boyne, in 1690. Just over a hundred years later, in 1800, the Act of Union was passed. The Irish were given 100 seats in the House of Commons and 32 seats in the House of Lords. Prime Minister William Pitt wished Catholics to be included and so, surprisingly, did the Protestants of •Ulster. This was the one big opportunity which the Government had of bringing Catholics and Protestants together in Ireland. But in those days Catholics were forbidden to sit in Parliament, and when King George III was asked for his consent, he refused. So, tragically, the opportunity was lost. Pitt resigned. Ireland was represented in the House of Commons only by the Protestants of the North. In the Catholic south, the elections could hardly be taken seriously.

Editor

Vocabulary

revenge	[ri'vendʒ]	somebody hits you. You hit them back. That is revenge.
declined	[di'klaind]	here: got smaller
crushed	[krʌʃt]	broke them (their rebellion) completely
Ulster	['ʌlstə]	ancient province in the north of Ireland where the Scottish Presbyterians settled, and the name by which Northern Ireland is now often known.

2. Catholic Ireland

Britain in the nineteenth century did nothing to improve Irish agriculture or to help the peasant tenants. Most of the big landlords spent nearly all their time in England. They became known as •"absentee landlords". Some of them were English. The peasants had miserable •plots of land on which they grew mostly potatoes. In fact, they depended on the potato. It was the only •nourishing food they could grow in sufficient quantities. Then suddenly in 1845 the potato was struck by a disease which destroyed practically the whole of Ireland's crop. It was the most terrible •disaster in Ireland's history. Neither the landlords nor the British government did much to help the •starving people. The disaster was called "the Great Hunger". Nobody knows for certain how many died, but it must have been at least a million and a quarter. Another million emigrated to England, the USA and all the English-speaking colonies.

The Irish Famine: Starving Peasants at a Workhouse Gate

The great Liberal leader, William Gladstone, was shocked by the misery of the Irish. In 1886 he introduced his first •Home Rule Bill for Ireland. Although his party had a majority in the House of Commons, not all Liberals were prepared to vote for even a semi-independent Ireland. British imperialism was then at its height, while Ireland was itself divided between the Catholic south and the Protestant north. When Lord Randolph Churchill, Winston Churchill's father, visited Ulster, he was welcomed by the Ulster Protestants with wild enthusiasm, especially when he used the slogan, "Ulster will fight. Ulster will be right." – meaning that Ulster men would fight rather than become part of a united self-governing Ireland.

Gladstone inroduced a second Home Rule Bill in 1893. The House of Commons passed it by only a few votes, but it was then rejected by the House of Lords.

Gladstone's Home Rule Bills did not offer the Irish complete independence. They offered a form of devolution. They would have given Ireland control over purely Irish affairs, but defence, foreign affairs and the economy would have remained in the hands of the Parliament at Westminster. It has been •claimed by some that if Ireland had been granted even this limited amount of self-government, Eire might still today be part of the United Kingdom. But the gulf between Protestant Ulster and the Catholic south was getting wider and wider, and the bitter hatred of the Catholic Irish for the British grew fiercer than ever. This hatred was felt, too, by the Irish who had emigrated to America.

Editor

Vocabulary

absentee	[ˌæbsənˈtiː]	landlords who were absent from, i.e. did not live on their estates
plots	[plɔts]	here: small pieces of land
nourishing	[ˈnʌriʃiŋ]	which gives strength to the body
disaster	[diˈzɑːstə]	a terrible event, usually with great loss of life (many dead)
starving	[stɑːviŋ]	dying of hunger
Home Rule		self-government
claimed	[kleimd]	here: declared, said

William Ewart Gladstone
(1809–1898)

3. Irish Hatred of England

a) Memory of the "Great Hunger"

The •famine left hatred behind. Between Ireland and England the memory of what was done and suffered has lain like a sword. Other famines followed, as other famines had gone before, but it is the terrible years of the Great Hunger which are remembered, and are only just beginning to be forgiven.
Time brought a just revenge. By the outbreak of the Second World war, (southern) Ireland was independent and she would not fight on England's side. Liberty and England did not appear to the Irish to have anything in common, and the *Free State remained neutral. Many thousands of Free State Irishmen volunteered, but the famous regiments of southern Ireland had ceased to exist, and the •"inexhaustable nursery of the finest soldiers" was no longer at England's service.
There was also more direct payment. Along the west coast are a number of graves of seamen of the British Navy and Merchant Service, representatives of many hundreds who were drowned off the coast of Ireland, because Irish ports were not open to British ships. From these innocents, in all probability knowing nothing of the past, who had never heard of the failure of the potato, •evictions, fever, •starvation, came payment in part for the price of the Great Hunger.

from "The Great Hunger", by Cecil Woodham-Smith

* Eire was originally called The Irish Free State (see. p. 90)

b) Driven from Home

Deep in the Irish heart, whether in Ireland itself or in England or in America, or in the colonies, survived the memory of ancient and terrible wrongs.
Sir James Sexton, whose father was •evicted in the 1840s by an •absentee landlord, and whose maternal grandparents had been driven out of Ireland into industrial Lancashire by the religious and political •persecutions following the Rebellion of 1798, wrote in his autobiography: "The story of those days of terror was handed on to the children of all who suffered their •agony; it spread all over the world and excited hatred in the mind of every Irishman and Irishwoman who heard it – a bitter, undying hatred of everything connected with Britain and the British".

from "English Saga", by Arthur Bryant

The Eviction of Irish Peasants

c) Irish American hatred of Britain

When Prince Charles toured the United States in the autumn of 1977, he was greeted in city after city by huge banners bearing the words, "WE HATE THE BRITISH". Until recently Irish Americans openly supplied arms to the IRA, even though the IRA was banned in the Irish Republic and had few sympathisers among the Catholics of the South.
His welcome in San Francisco was particularly unfriendly. The small crowd was dominated by a large group of Irish Americans who waved Irish Republican flags, and brought to their demonstration an ancient bus covered with banners which read "Stop killing Irish children," "Brits out. peace in." "Stop the torture, Charlie!"

Editor

Vocabulary

famine	[ˈfæmin]	when there is not enough food for the people and they begin to starve; famines are usually caused by disasters: droughts, floods, war etc.
inexhaustable	[ˌinigˈzɔːstəbl]	goes on for ever
evictions	[i(ː)ˈvikʃənz]	noun of "to evict", the landlords evicted peasants from their homes, i.e., drove them out, forced them to leave

starvation	[stɑːˈveiʃən]	dying of hunger
evicted	[i(ː)ˈviktid]	see "evictions", (above)
absentee landlord	[ˈæbsənti ˈlænlɔːd]	see Vocabulary p. 85
persecutions	[ˌpəːsiˈkjuːʃənz]	actions which make life difficult and dangerous, i.e., the persecution of the Protestants by the Catholics; or the Catholics by the Protestants
agony		extreme suffering, or pain

4. The First World War and the Dublin Rebellion

The difference in attitude between the Protestant and Catholic Irish was underlined during the First World War. The Ulster volunteers fought with tremendous courage at the Battle of the Somme and suffered •appalling losses. They felt that they had shown how loyal they were to the British connection and remembered the Somme not with horror, but with pride. Two hundred thousand Catholic Irish, most of them nationalists, also fought at the Somme, and in other murderous battles. They volunteered, and they obeyed orders and did not •mutiny. But these battles, in which they fought side by side with their "oppressors" did not become part of their history. A much deeper memory for them was the Dublin Rebellion on Easter Monday, 1916 – a few months before the Battle of the Somme. Yet the rebellion was a tragic failure:

The plans for an •uprising throughout the country in 1916 went badly wrong and even at their best their hope of success depended on moral rather than military considerations. A •cargo of arms from Germany, timed to arrive just before the rising, was captured and sent to the bottom of the sea. The secrecy with which a small group of leaders had made their plans caused a muddle of orders and counterorders, the delaying of the rising by one day and a breakdown in communications. It was only in Dublin that an effective fighting force turned out, on Easter Monday, and even then it was below strength; nonetheless the authorities were taken by surprise, and the volunteers and Citizen Army seized the centre of the city and held it with great courage for a bloody week against the British Army.
At last, after •shelling and burning had reduced their strong-points, the rebels •surrendered, leaving central Dublin in ruins, many soldiers and civilians dead, and Ireland changed. In the early days of May, morning after morning, the leaders of the rising were shot in Kilmainham prison. The shock to the population who had known these men was horrible beyond belief.
Asquith, the then Prime Minister, stopped the military commander in Dublin from shooting his prisoners, and announced to the House of Commons on May 11th: "The Government has come to the conclusion that the system under which Ireland has been governed has completely broken down. The only satisfactory alternative in their judgment is the creation at the earliest possible moment of an Irish Government responsible to the Irish people".

from "Divided Ulster", by Liam de Parr

Vocabulary

appalling	[ə'pɔːliŋ]	terrible (but slightly stronger)
mutiny	['mjuːtini]	when soldiers refuse to obey their officers
uprising	[ʌpraiziŋ]	rebellion
cargo	['kɑːgəu]	ships carry cargoes of cars, sugar, food of all kinds etc., etc.
shelling	[ʃeliŋ]	firing heavy guns at
surrendered	[sə'rendəd]	stopped fighting and gave themselves up to the enemy

5. Violence and terror in Ireland

In the General Election of December 1918, the extreme left-wing party in Ireland, Sinn Fein, swept the moderate nationalists off the political map. The new Irish members of Parliament did not get to Westminster, but stayed in Dublin. They •proclaimed themselves the first Parliament of Ireland and published a statement of their general aims, which began:

"We declare in the words of the Irish Republican Proclamation the right of the people of Ireland to the ownership of Ireland, and in the language of our first President, Padraig MacPhiarais (Gaelic for Patrick Pearse) we declare that the nation's sovereignty •extends not only to all men and women of the Nation, but to all its material possessions, all the wealth-producing processes within the nation, and with him we declare, that all right to private property must be •subordinated to the public right and welfare.
"We declare that we desire our country to be ruled in accordance with the principles of Liberty, Equality and Justice for all ..."

Before long the Sinn Fein movement had developed into a fierce guerilla war with the British, who regarded them as rebels. The fighting on both sides was •merciless:

British officers were •dragged from their beds by masked •assassins and •butchered in front of their wives, an imprisoned Lord Mayor starved himself to death to •shame the Saxon despot, and Sinn Fein gunmen (who now began to call themselves the Irish Republican Army – IRA) maintained a rival and forbidden administration, with their own parliament, army, police and courts of justice, •defying those of the imperial government, with whom they fought a ceaseless and bloody war.

from "English Saga", by Arthur Bryant

Vocabulary

proclaimed themselves	[prə'kleimd ðəm'selvz]	announced that they were, publicly called themselves
extends	[iks'tendz]	stretches out. Here: the word has the sense of "includes everything, not only ..."

subordinated	[sə'bɔːdineitid]	the right to private property is much less important than the public right. The public right to property must always be put before the private right
merciless	['məːsilis]	without any pity
dragged	[drægd]	pulled by force
assassin	[ə'sæsin]	murderer
butcher	['butʃə]	kill in a merciless way. Usually suggests large numbers of people killed, i.e. Everyone in the town was butchered.
shame	[ʃeim]	make some one feel ashamed, guilty
defying	[di'faiiŋ]	refusing to obey, having nothing to do with

6. A Free Ireland is born – and so is the IRA

The British Government, not knowing what else to do, then introduced into Ireland a police force of ex-army adventurers, chosen for their •toughness. They were called the "Black and Tans", because of their uniform. They wore a khaki jacket and a black cap. The Black and Tans were told to "raise hell in Irish villages". But this was too much for the British public who, although they did not like the Irish, were opposed to any form of terrorism, nationalistic or official. They protested strongly and forced the Government to put an end to these •legalised acts of brutality.
In 1921 the Liberal Prime Minister, Lloyd George, offered the Irish self-government and •Dominion status. The offer was accepted, but it had come too late. It did not satisfy some nationalists, who wished to cut off all ties with Britain. A few years later the Irish Free State, as it was then called, became a Republic and at the same time left the Commonwealth.
But first the new Irish Government had to fight the extreme republicans and their army, the IRA. The extremists no longer had the sympathy of the Irish people. The Government won a senseless and bloody civil war, but the IRA did not consider themselves defeated and it was not the last that either the Irish or the British were to see of them.
Meanwhile, •Ulster had refused to join the free Ireland. They wanted to remain British, and they threatened to take up arms if they were forced to unite with the Catholic south.

Editor

Vocabulary

toughness	[tʌfnis]	here: having no feelings of fear, or of pity
legalised	['liːgʌlaizd]	made legal, accepted as lawful by the Government
Dominion status	[də'minjən 'steitəs]	having complete freedom, but remaining a member of the Commonwealth
Ulster	['ʌlstə]	see Vocabulary p. 83

Lloyd George, Prime Minister from 1916 to 1922

B. Fanatical Ulster

1. The Fight to Stay British

Ireland was England's first colony, and this must never be forgotten when considering Irish history. Ever since the first English soldiers set foot on Irish •soil eight centuries ago, there has been much misery and •bloodshed.
Most people see the problem of Ireland as religious. Everyone agrees that the Irish people can be divided into two clearly cut religious groups, Catholics and Protestants. Everyone agrees that religious intolerance has helped to keep these two groups apart. But historians consider the problem of Ireland to be essentially colonial. The troubles of modern Ireland go back to the sixteenth and seventeenth centuries when, under the Tudor monarchs and later under Cromwell, English and Scottish Protestants were sent to Ulster as settlers. Their main duty was to keep watch over the rebellious Catholic natives.
It is significant that the violence which broke out in Northern Ireland in 1969 began on August 12th. This is the day on which, every year, Protestants celebrate with marching and the beating of drums the defeat of the Catholic army which •besieged them in Londonderry 200 years ago. Ulster Protestants celebrate other victories, particularly the Battle of the Boyne and the crushing

Rioting in Londonderry

of the great Catholic revolution. These celebrations never fail to anger the Catholics.

At the end of the eighteenth century Protestant extremists formed a society which they called, in honour of William of Orange, the "Orange Society". The object of this society was to make sure that Protestant Loyalists (i. e. Protestants loyal to the British Crown) never lost control in Ulster. Orangemen throughout their history have always been militant. They have caused frequent riots, and they have fought Catholics at the slightest provocation. It was they who •wrecked Lloyd George's plan for a unified Ireland in 1921. They armed themselves and threatened to fight rather than become part of the Catholic south.

When in 1922 the Catholic south became an independent republic (Eire), the Protestant north remained part of the United Kingdom. In Northern Ireland, or Ulster as it is often called, it was quite impossible to separate completely Catholics from Protestants. Whole Catholic communities were left behind – like islands in a Protestant sea. They became a minority, a large minority, since about a third of Ulster is Catholic. Few of these Catholics wanted to move to the south. They were getting better jobs and more money in the north. Yet they were not satisfied.

Protestants were given the best jobs and the best houses. Some bosses even refused to employ Catholics. As for the voting system, it has always been unjust. In Londonderry Catholics •outnumber Protestants two to one, but the city council was always controlled by Protestants.

Northern Ireland sends twelve representatives to the Parliament at Westminster but unlike Scotland and Wales, it also had a parliament of its own, called "Stormont". Stormont had the right to deal with all home affairs without inteference from Westminster. Stormont was, in fact, the first case of devolution in the United Kingdom. But ever since it was founded in 1922, it was controlled by one party, the Ulster Unionists, who were all Protestants. Since they were always in power, the Unionists had complete control of the police, the Royal Ulster Constabulary. This disturbed, angered and sometimes frightened the Catholics. Until 1969 the RUC was the only police force in the United Kingdom to carry guns. During the riots of 1969, some policemen used their guns and several Catholics were killed. At the •request of the British government the RUC were •disarmed and British troops were sent out to Ulster to keep the peace. They were welcomed by the Catholics.

•Moderate Catholics at this time were not demanding revolutionary changes in Stormont. They were demanding only their civil rights (i.e. equality with the Protestants in all branches of society). The leaders of the Civil Rights movement were non-violent, and they had the support of many moderate Protestants. They believed that they could •persuade Stormont by peaceful demonstrations. They organised their marches before the serious riots began, and they were stoned and beaten up by Protestant extremists. In one battle Protestants used guns and killed six people. British troops now took a tougher line, but the Catholics soon accused them of taking sides with the Protestants.

from "Britain Today", by Richard Musman

Vocabulary

soil	[sɔil]	earth
bloodshed	[ˈblʌdʃed]	killings and woundings
significant	[sigˈnifikənt]	here: of special interest
besieged	[biˈsiːdʒd]	surrounded the city and made it impossible for any one to get out
wrecked	[rekt]	ruined, made useless
outnumber	[autˈnʌmbə]	there are twice as many Catholics as Protestants
at the request of	[riˈkwest]	when the British government asked
disarmed	[diˈɑːmd]	had their weapons (guns) taken from them
moderate	[ˈmɔdərit]	avoiding extremes
persuade	[pəˈsweid]	here: make Stormont give them what they wanted

2. The Irish Republican Army – IRA

Many people claim that the tougher attitude of the army was made unavoidable by the behaviour of the most extreme of all anti-unionist organisations, the IRA (Irish Republican Army). The IRA's object has always been the unification of Ireland – not a union under the present Catholic government of Eire, but a union planned and run by the political organisation of the IRA itself. The IRA, as we have seen, has a long •record of violence. During the second world war it formed an alliance with the Nazis, and it is now said to be largely Marxist. Until 1969 it had little support in Ulster.

It was the riots of 1969 which gave the IRA their chance. The bitter people of the Catholic ghettos of Belfast and Londonderry welcomed the IRA, and the IRA bombers and gunmen knew that they could hide in these ghettos without fear of being given away. The people of the ghettos accepted them as their champions. At the same time they were afraid of them. It was dangerous to have relations with the "other side". There were "executions". Boys had their knee-caps shot off. Two girls were •tarred and feathered for going out with British soldiers.

When the terrorism began on a large scale in 1970 the IRA were split into two rival groups, the Official IRA and the Provisional IRA. The object of both groups was the breakdown of society, the •removal of the British army, the starting of a civil war between Catholics and Protestants and the destruction of Stormont.

The methods of the Provisional IRA were brutal. They planted bombs in crowded shopping centres, sometimes with awful results. They also killed soldiers and policemen. They destroyed countless buildings.

In February 1972, a new Loyalist organisation called "Vanguard" was formed by a former right-wing Stormont minister, William Craig. Its aim was to defend Stormont and keep the Ulster Protestants in control. It was violently opposed to direct rule from Westminster and yet wanted Ulster to remain part of the United Kingdom.

Explosion in Belfast

In an attempt to put an end to all the violence and misery, the British government took over full control of Northern Ireland, Stormont was suspended, at first for one year, and the Prime Minister and the cabinet resigned. An Englishman, William Whitelaw, was sent to Belfast as Secretary of State for Northern Ireland.

The violence continued throughout 1970–73. The British soldiers were now hated by Catholics and Protestants alike. In 1973 representatives of the British and Irish (Eire) governments and the more moderate Protestant and Catholic leaders met at Sunningdale in England. They agreed to set up a power-sharing government of Protestants and Catholics in Northern Ireland. But the extremists on both sides refused to accept power-sharing. The Loyalists were particularly furious because they suspected that power-sharing would be the first step towards a United Ireland in which Protestants would be a minority. This is their constant fear, although Protestants have never been •persecuted by the people of the Irish Republic.

In 1974 the Loyalist Workers Council called a general strike. This put an end to the power-sharing government and forced the British government to •reintroduce direct rule from Westminster. Now militant Protestant groups showed that they could be as violent as the IRA.

In the same year IRA terrorists came to Britain, planting bombs in pubs, hotels, tube stations, anywhere where there were crowds of people. No warning was given and many people were killed or wounded, but by the end of 1975 the police had caught most of the bombers.
The bitter opposition of the Protestants to the idea of power-sharing with the Catholic minority made a solution impossible. So the bombings and killings went on. By 1976 hardly a day passed without Catholic killing Protestant, or Protestant killing Catholic.
In the summer of 1976 the Women's Peace Movement was founded. There were soon thousands of followers, Protestants as well as Catholics. They called for an end to violence from *all* sides. The violence went on, but more and more terrorists on both sides were caught. There were no longer so many places where they could hide.

from "Britain Today", by Richard Musman

In 1977 the two women who founded the Peace Movement were awarded the Nobel Peace Prize, but the Peace Movement does not seem to be having the same effect any more. The novelty has worn off, and it is said that there is no longer harmony among the leaders.

Vocabulary

record	[ˈrekɔːd]	here: history
tarred and feathered	[tɑːd ənd feðəd]	covered with tar (Teer) which is then covered with feathers
removal	[riˈmuːvəl]	noun of "to remove"; to take away
persecuted	[ˈpəːsikjuːtid]	treated with cruelty, made to suffer
reintroduce	[riːˌintrəˈdjuːs]	introduce again

Nobel Prize for Mairead Corrigan (left) and Betty Williams

3. What plans do the IRA have for a new Northern Ireland?

This is a •satirical •account of how the IRA might organise Ulster if ever they got control of the province. It was published in Punch, one of the most famous humorous and satirical journals in the English-speaking world. The new IRA Government would, of course, take away as much as it could from Belfast, the present capital, which is mainly Protestant, and give it to Londonderry, which is mainly Catholic (many members of the IRA had – and still have – their •hideouts in Londonderry).

There are numerous indirect references to IRA practices in the article: "Missing kneecaps": the IRA sometimes shot off the kneecaps of their sympathisers if they thought they were disloyal, or if they were seen in the company of Protestants.

"Armaments": the IRA hid their bombs, guns, ammunition, etc. in houses both in Britain and Ireland.

"Commission in the IRA": being an "officer" in the IRA.

"Queen's University": the University of Belfast.

"Finance": the IRA have been getting much of their money from Irish Americans, their "housing policy" and "transport policy" should be obvious!

Transport: They place bombs under parked cars, and set them to go off when the engine is started. They also frequently steal cars.

Our Plans for a New Northern Ireland

by the IRA

When the British Army is finally driven out of Ireland, when the people are allowed once again to rule their own land, there will be a need for far-sighted policies and firm government. We believe we are damned well going to supply both. Here is our vision of the future in detail. When you have read our •manifesto, please •swallow or destroy.

HEALTH

Hospital services will be provided by the State. We won't bother with highly expensive treatment for rare diseases; instead, the health service will deal with the commonest troubles such as missing kneecaps, bomb splinters, blast damage, stopping breathing and dying.

DISCRIMINATION

It will be unlawful to tell short silly jokes about any race or creed.

7 Musman, United Kingdom? PB (41035)

INDUSTRY

There will be a heavy investment programme in Londonderry, industrial capital of the north. The old-fashioned industries of Belfast will slowly be allowed to run down over a period of several weeks and the majority of the population will be given the opportunity to rehouse themselves, in Britain, for instance, where most of them came from in the first place.

There will also be a solid home-based armaments industry. Until now we have depended far too much on imports from East Europe, which is far too expensive as well as being the very devil to get into the country. We already have the beginnings of a national armaments industry, but it keeps getting found.

Industry will be run by the Industrial Wing of the IRA.

EDUCATION

The Educational Wing of the IRA, in its special new uniform of berets, green •camouflage and light weight boots, will take charge of all schools and colleges. Emphasis will be on Irish history, Irish geography, Irish, religious instruction and discipline. A commission in the IRA will be accepted as adequate qualification for entering Queen's University, which will be renamed.

DEFENCE

The standing army is, of course, the IRA. The naval strength of the new Northern Ireland will be the Marine Wing of the IRA, formerly known as Belfast shipyards. The air force will be known as the Wing of the IRA.

TRANSPORT

The main form of transport will be by car. Anybody's, it doesn't matter, but for God's sake look under it first.

FINANCE

The main source of income will remain as before, and this explains the unusual necessity of keeping the Financial Wing of the IRA in the Irish areas of America.

HOUSING

The Housing Wing of the IRA intends to improve the housing picture progressively. This will be done by blowing up fewer and fewer houses every year.

FOREIGN POLICY

We •pledge ourselves to have no foreign policy. We will have our own policy and be damned to the foreigners.

FOREIGN POLICY

It has just been pointed out to us what foreign policy means. Well now, in that case we shall set up a Russian naval base in Strangford Lough and see how the British like that for starters. We shall discourage Chinese take away restaurants, as it's hard enough trying to hit a restaurant that's standing still.

HOME POLICY
The Home Wing of the IRA will of course be making immediate moves to reunite Ireland so that we can be under one government. We will however be safeguarding the Protestant minority in Northern Ireland and will be giving them exactly the same rights and protection as they gave us before. *That* should be good for a laugh.

CURRENCY
The Electrical Wing of the IRA intends to stick to the normal 250 volts.

from "Punch", January 21st 1976

Vocabulary

satirical	[sə'tirikəl]	adj. of satire
account	[ə'kaunt]	story, description
hide-out		place where you can hide with little danger of being discovered
manifesto	[.mæniəfestəu]	public declaration of policy or programme of a political party
swallow	['swɔləu]	cause food (or mainfestos!) to pass down one's throat into one's stomach
camouflage	['kæmuflɑ:ʒ]	*Tarnung*
pledge ourselves	[pledʒ .auə'selvz]	give a firm promise
Strangford Lough	[lɔk]	"Lough" is an Anglo-Irish word. It has the same meaning as the Scottish "loch". Strangford Lough is just south of Belfast.

4. Militant Protestants

A militant Protestant leader, called the Reverend Ian Paisley, as well as other militant "Loyalists", have made things more and more difficult for the British Government and for those in Ulster who want peace. By 1977, ironically, some "Loyalists" were talking of independence. Paisley called a general strike, demanding stronger measures against the IRA, and the return of Stormont. The strike failed, though Paisly remained as popular and powerful as ever. Direct rule continued from Westminster and Stormont was not recalled. About the only thing Ulster local Councils were responsible for was the emptying of dustbins and the cleaning of the streets.
Even if the demand of the "Loyalists" for independence became stronger, it is very unlikely that the British would ever give complete freedom to Northern Ireland – not even if a majority of the population voted for it. For Ulster is different from Scotland and Wales. It has a Catholic minority that still needs protection against the Protestants. Almost everyone agrees that this is a task for the British Government – certainly not for the IRA. Except for a few Catholic MPs, independence is what the Catholics in Northern Ireland dread most. And they do not want a return to devolution either, unless they are allowed their fair share of power. In 1977 there still seemed to be no solution to the problems of Northern Ireland. In fact, there were certain aspects about the Reverend Ian Paisley's strike which alarmed a good many people ...

According to a mysterious document sent anonymously to three well-known Loyalists four months ago, plans for the strike had been laid at a series of meetings last year. The document, which reads like an intelligence report, claims that, as long ago as last September, the •objective had in fact, been to •stage a putsch. Certainly extremely detailed plans had been made to set up organisations of a governmental nature. At one headquarters I happened to visit in the early days of the strike, the entire first floor of a housing block had been taken over as a co-ordinating centre for the provision of transport, food and fuel supplies when normal services collapsed.

Up to now, the idea of independence has been suggested by a strange combination of Loyalist paramilitaries and small businessmen, though both Paisley and Baird, the two leaders of extreme Protestantism, deny they have any ambitions in that direction. But independence was one of the ideas discussed in the so-called "peace talks" between a former Dublin politician and a well-known Northern Ireland lawyer.

Although the "peace talks" have brought a •torrent of denials from Loyalist •paramilitary leaders, there clearly have been discussions. But the idea of an independent Ulster frightens to death many Catholics.

from "As you were in Ulster", by Jeremy Paxman
the Listener, May 26th 1977

Three days after the start of the Loyalist strike in Ulster, the following birth notice appeared in one of the papers:

> Brooks – Loyalist Councillor Michael and Mrs Yvonne Brooks rejoice in the birth of a Loyalist daughter, Catherine Sarah, a sister for Loyalist son, John. Another supporter for the stoppage, and another vote for Daddy.
>
> Up Paisley. No surrender!
> Praise God from whom all blessings flow!

Vocabulary

objective	[əb'dʒektiv]	aim, purpose
stage a putsch		organise, arrange an armed rebellion (German "Putsch" has become part of the English language).
torrent of denials	['tɔrant əv di'naiəlz]	a flood, a huge number of denials (i.e. we never said anything about it, we deny that we ...)
paramilitary	['pærə'militri]	not part of the regular army, but with some military training

C. Violence Doesn't Pay

1. Gwynfor Evans Discusses Ireland's Fight for Freedom

Ireland is the country which has most deeply influenced Welsh nationalism during the last three generations. Its freedom is often quoted as evidence of the successful use of violence. In my opinion the history of Ireland is a warning against the use of violence in the cause of nationalism. Although non-violent methods would not have provided the country with the inspiration of the noble heroes who led the 1916 Easter Rising, I believe if they had been used, Ireland would be a freer and happier land today, more united and more Irish. Certainly there was a magnificence in the Easter Rising, but it lay in the suffering and the sacrifice, not in the violence. If there were less Irishmen ready to live than to shoot and die for Ireland, it was because of the uncritical Irish acceptance of the custom that violence is alone heroic and effective. This gave the men of violence and their methods a status which has tended to overshadow the aims for which they fought. The continued glorification of violence in Ireland poisons the situation north and south of the Border; it is the soil in which the IRA and the UDA flourish.

1916 led in Ireland to 1922. Irish violence against the British led to Irish violence against the Irish. The Civil War of 1922 created bitterness within the country. Ireland has not known the brightness of a new dawn which has come with freedom to so many countries ... No doubt the measure of self-government it had achieved was a little fuller, but how heart-breaking the cost. If it had relied on non-violent methods, it would have achieved more a few years later. If the flash of brilliance, the joy of living, and the confident experiment have been absent from the Irish scene since 1922, this is largely due, I think, to the civil war. The joy of the victorious fight against the British was followed by the terrible tragedy of Irish self-defeat.

from "Non-Violent Nationalism", a lecture given by Gwynfor Evans in 1973

Exercises

A. The Long Fight for Freedom

1. Irish Misery p. 83
   1. Religion has always bedevilled (ruined) relationships between the Irish and the English. Study the text carefully and quote as many examples as you can of the folly and terrible intolerance of the English.
   2. If William Pitt had had his way, why might the whole history of the British Isles have been different?
   3. In the 18th century the monarch still had some authority. What did he do in the case of the Irish which caused Pitt to resign?
   4. Why were the Irish MPs representing the North of Ireland able to take their seats in the House of Commons?
   5. Is there any hostility between Catholics and Protestants in your country?

2. Catholic Ireland p. 84
   1. Explain the meaning of "absentee landlord".
   2. Explain the significance (importance) of 1845 in Irish and British history.
   3. Was William Gladstone a great man in your opinion? If you think so, explain why.
   4. There are several reasons why Home Rule for Ireland would have been impossible, or at least problematical. What reasons can you find in the text?

3. Irish hatred of England p. 86
   1. In what direct way did Britain suffer as a result of Irish hatred?
   2. Driven from home: write in simple language the meaning of Sir James Sexton's story, beginning: "The story of those days ..." p. 86
   3. Irish American hatred of Britain p. 87:
      1. Do people in your country think that it is right or wrong to supply arms to the IRA? Is America criticised in your press for having done this? What do you think personally?
      2. How much do you know about the IRA? Write down what you already know before you read any of the texts which follow.

4. The First World War and the Dublin Rebellion (Easter 1916) p. 88
   1. Compare the Protestant and Catholic Irish attitudes towards the First World War.
   2. Write a short essay on the Dublin Rebellion. Here are some guide-lines: Things went wrong from the first: how? But in Dublin there was fighting. Authorities taken by surprise. Who did they fight in Dublin? Courage of Citizen Army. What shocked the Irish public? Attitude of British Government. What did the Irish gain out of the Rebellion, even though it was crushed?

5. Violence and terror in Ireland p. 89
   Summarize the proclamation of the first Irish Republic

6. A Free Ireland is born – and so is the IRA
   1. The British took military action. What form did it take?
   2. 1. "This was too much for the British public". Comment on this phrase.
      2. What was the result of this protest?
   3. 1. What happened after the Irish were granted independence?
      2. How did Ulster make things more difficult?

B. Fanatical Ulster

1. The fight to stay British p. 92
   1. Illustrate the phrase, "Ireland was England's first colony".
   2. In what way does the history of Ireland differ from that of Scotland or Wales?
   3. Explain the significance of the "Orangemen". How did they help to make Ireland a divided country?

4. Select phrases from the text which show that Ulster has never been a true democracy, and that it was really a one-party state.
5. Who, in your opinion, started the troubles in Northern Ireland?

2. The Irish Republican Army (IRA) p. 94
   1. What sort of unification did the IRA want?
   2. What is a ghetto?
   3. What was the object of both groups of the IRA, Provisional and Official? Which group took charge of the attacks on the Protestants?
   4. What was the object of the new Loyalist group, Vanguard? What did it not want at any cost?
   5. British soldiers were now in Northern Ireland. They were hated by Catholics and Protestants alike. What did your newspapers have to say about the presence of British troops in Ulster? Do you think they went there as oppressors? What do you think would happen if they were withdrawn?
   6. What did the Loyalists do to spoil any chance of a peaceful solution?
   7. Using the answers to the questions above as guide-lines, write an essay on the state of Northern Ireland between 1970 and 1974. Your essay should not be more than half the length of the passage.
   8. In 1974 the terrorists came to Britain, and about 50 people were killed, mostly by bombs hidden in public houses. What is your attitude towards urban guerillas or terrorists?
   9. Do you think the Women's Peace Movement will have much effect in putting an end to the terror?

3. Our Plans for a New Northern Ireland p. 97
   1. Do you find this article from Punch funny? Can you see the satire?
   2. 1. Explain the significance of:
      HEALTH – hospital services: ... won't bother with rare diseases, instead ... with the commonest troubles such as missing kneecaps, splinters, blast damage, stopping breathing and dying.
      2. INDUSTRY – We already have the makings of a (home-based) armaments industry, but it keeps getting found out. Can you explain?
      3. TRANSPORT – Where is the humour here? It is very bitter humour. Why?
      4. HOUSING – The IRA intends to improve the housing situation by blowing up fewer and fewer houses each week. What is *Punch* referring to?
      5. FOREIGN POLICY – ... We shall discourage Chinese take-away restaurants, as it's hard enough trying to hit them standing still. Explain the joke.
      6. HOME POLICY – We will be safeguarding the Protestant minority in Northern Ireland and will be giving them exactly the same rights and protection as they gave us. Who is *Punch* satirising here?

4. Militant Protestants p. 99
   1. Give a pen picture of your impression of a "militant Protestant".
   2. What is Stormont?
   3. Why do the Catholics not want the return of Stormont? Complete the sentence: The Catholics would only agree to the return of Stormont if ...

4. Complete these sentences:
   1. Paisley called a strike because ...
   2. The British would never give Northern Ireland independence, not even if ...
   3. The mysterious document suggested that ...
5. The British would never consider giving Ulster independence. Does this strike you as being authoritarian, or undemocratic, or is there in this case a justifiable reason (a reason you can agree with)?

C. Violence Doesn't Pay

1. Gwynfor Evans discusses Ireland's fight for freedom p. 101
   Write a critical appreciation of this piece by Gwynfor Evans. Here are some guide-lines: Was violence justified in the struggle against the British? – Is it better to live than to shoot and die? – Praise of the Easter Rebellion, but ... – His opinion of the glorification of violence by the Irish – Effect on atmosphere in Ireland today – Would have achieved freedom more easily without violence – The tragedy that happened in 1922 – The tragedy of self-defeat.

Violence in Belfast

V. The Politics of Devolution

A. Things as they are (or were) before Devolution

1. How much self-rule have Scotland, Northern Ireland, and Wales got now (1979)?

1. **Wales:** has practically no self-rule at all, except through local government. There is a Secretary of State for Wales, a Welshman appointed by the Prime Minister whose main task is to keep an eye on Government policy as it affects Wales.

2. **Northern Ireland:** now ruled directly from Westminster through a Secretary of State for Ireland, who is not an Irishman. Formerly had a parliament of its own, called "Stormont" which looked after home affairs. No prospect of Stormont being restored until majority of Protestants agree to power-sharing with Catholics.

3. **Scotland:** Very few people realise how much is being done by Scots for Scots. Scotland has its own Free (Presbyterian) Church of Scotland, its own traditional legal system (law courts) and control of its own police forces, its own Departments of Education, of Agriculture and Fisheries, of Home Affairs and Health, of Scottish Development (town and country planning, roads, local government etc.) and has considerable control over Scottish economic planning.
   A Secretary of State, appointed by the Prime Minister, is responsible for these departments, called generally the Scottish Office. The day by day work of the Scottish Office is carried out in a large modern building in Edinburgh. English ministers of •equivalent departments have no say in the work or decisions of the Scottish departments.
   Many Scots do not consider government by the Scottish Office to be self-rule at all. The Secretary of State for Scotland, although always a Scot, is frequently not the sort of man the Scots would have chosen themselves. Besides, the •post is regarded by ministers as one of the least important of Cabinet appointments, which does not inspire the Scots with much confidence or enthusiasm. He also spends more time at Westminster than in Scotland.

Editor

Vocabulary

equivalent	[iˈkwivələnt]	here: English departments which have the same duties as the Scottish departments
post	[pəust]	here: job

B. The Part Played by the Different Political Parties in the Devolution Debate

1. Those for and those against the Devolution Bill

During 1976, before the Government's Devolution Bill was introduced, there was a debate in the House of Commons. This debate showed quite clearly that the bill was going to have a very difficult journey indeed. There were so many different views on what form Devolution should take. At one extreme the SNP and Plaid Cymru demanded complete self-government. At the other extreme many Conservatives were against any kind of Devolution, while a strong minority of Labour MPs were also against Devolution and in favour of a united Labour Party, composed of English, Scots and Welsh within the United Kingdom.

Many Scottish Labour MPs, however, warned the Party that unless the Devolution Bill was passed, Labour might lose so many Scottish votes at the next election that they might also lose all their Scottish seats. If that happened there might never be another Labour Government at Westminster, for the Labour Party depends to a very large extent on the votes of the Scots and Welsh to win elections for them.

There were other Labour rebels. In 1976 two Scottish Labour MPs left the Labour Party and joined a new break-away Scottish Labour Party which, like the SNP, wants independence or at least self-government for Scotland.

There is an uncomfortable feeling among many people that Political Parties are using Devolution as a means of fighting each other. There are Welshmen, Scots and Englishmen who are worried and even disgusted by the game the two major parties are playing. Scottish and Welsh politicians, they claim, are more interested in saving their seats at Westminster than in looking after the interests of their •constituents. Others, less cynical, accuse the politicians of being blinded by party loyalty.

Herein lies the reason why the Labour Government failed to pass the Devolution Bill in February, 1977. There were deliberate delaying tactics not only on the part of the Conservative Opposition, but also on the part of Labour rebels. Nonetheless there was a genuine desire on the part of many Devolutionists and anti-Devolutionists to save the United Kingdom from breaking up. Some thought it could be done by supporting separate Assemblies for Scotland and Wales. Others thought these Assemblies would be the first step towards independence, especially in Scotland.

Editor

Vocabulary

constituents	[kən'stitjuənts]	voters within an MP's constituency (the district he represents)

Devolution – Yes or No

2. Why the Labour Government did not fall after the failure of the first Devolution Bill – the part played by the Liberals

After the failure of the Devolution Bill in 1977 everyone expected the Government to resign. It was a great blow to the Conservatives that they did not. The Government survived only because the tiny Liberal Party under its Scottish leader, David Steel, offered to support them – on condition that the Liberals were always consulted before any new bill was introduced.

The Liberals' views on Devolution were far more generous than those of the two main parties. Liberals would have been prepared to offer the Scots and Welsh a much larger measure of self-government. They wanted a form of federation. They would even have considered giving the Scots 50% of the North Sea oil •revenues. The Labour Government had no intention of going as far as that, but they knew they had to consider some of the Liberal demands if they wished to stay in office.

At the end of 1977 the Labour Government decided to introduce two separate Bills, one for Wales and the other for Scotland. Few people believed that they would succeed.

Editor

Vocabulary

revenues	[ˈrevinjuz]	money received (from oil)

3. The Government passes the Devolution Bills

a) In the summer of 1978 the Government was successful. Parliament passed the two Devolution Bills, one for Scotland and the other for Wales (see p. 5)

There is one very important difference between the Welsh Bill and the Scottish Bill: the Scottish Assembly in Edinburgh will have power to make its own laws on "devolved" matters (i.e. matters for which they will be responsible), but the Welsh Assembly in Cardiff will only have the power to administer, or carry out, existing laws on "devolved" matters.
Here are the chief "devolved" matters which are to be the responsibility of the Welsh and Scottish Assemblies:

1) education, including the arts, libraries, and sport, but *not* the universieties.
2) health and Social Services
3) water services
4) local Government
5) ancient monuments and historic buildings
6) environment, including pollution, new towns, the countryside and industrial sites
7) development and industry, agricultural land (including forestry and fisheries)
8) housing
9) tourism
10) •betting and •licensing
11) •charities
12) shop hours
13) fire services

b) Why the Nationalists were disappointed with the Devolution Bills

The Government at Westminster was to keep control over the finances, and over all important matters concerning trade and industry. The Bills gave no power to the two Assemblies to raise their own taxes. This is a power that the SNP particularly want, but the Government claimed that it would be too difficult and complicated to have three separate tax systems in the U.K. Neither the SNP nor Plaid Cymru were pleased about the terms of the referendum (see p. 5).

Editor

Vocabulary

betting	['betiŋ]	I bet you £10 my horse will win the race.
licensing	['laisənsiŋ]	permission given by local government to run a pub, a club, drive a motor-car etc. Every motorist has a driving licence.

charities [ˈtʃærɪtɪz] There are thousands of charities big and small in Britain – charities to help all kinds of people and all kinds of animals. People give up their free time to work for charities and they accept no pay. Many millions of pounds are collected each year for charities.

C. The Political Parties in Scotland and Wales

1. Conservatives and Labour

a) The failure of the Tories

The Labour Party are desperately worried about the state of the Tory Party in both Scotland and Wales. They would rather have the Tories as the opposition than the SNP or Plaid Cymru.

Between 1900 and 1950 the Conservative Party had, more often than not, a majority both of seats and votes in Scotland. Since then it has been downhill all the way.

Latest General Election Statistics in Scotland, October 1974*

	Cons.	Lab.	Lib.	SNP
% of votes:	24%	36,3%	8.3%	30%
No. of seats:	16	41	3	11

* See footnote p. 64

A story is being told that in one •constituency, held by Labour, the Labour agent sent his helpers out to deliver Tory leaflets the day before the poll. The leaflets told the voters to vote Tory. The Tories, the leaflet said, are the only real anti-Socialist party. The Labour agent was afraid that if any more votes moved from the Tories to the SNP, Labour would lose the seat. Labour won – just. But with 35 constituencies where the Nationalists are now second to Labour, the future health of the Conservative Party is, or ought to be, of great concern to the Labour Party.

b) Tory candidates in Scotland are not suitable (see IIC p. 37)

The trouble with the Tories in Scotland is that their members have rarely had much in common with the middle-class people who make up their constituencies. They have consisted almost entirely of •"lairds" – lawyers, farmers, military men. These lairds tended to be English in education and religion ...

Many of these lairds live in England, have English accents, and do not feel •at ease with the Scots. Many of them are, in fact, Anglo-Scots, of which there are a vast number in England now (of all classes).

However, in February 1974 a few Tories were elected who were clearly of a new type – youngish, reasonably progressive and having some sort of likeness to their •constituents ... "At last," one of them told me, "we seemed to be getting the sort of people we need, but we were ten years too late ..."

In the elections for the local councils in 1977, the Tories had some surprising successes in Scotland. The SNP did well, but not quite as well as they had expected.

c) The state of the Parties in Wales

Latest General Election Statistics in Wales, 1974*

	Cons.	Lab.	Lib.	Plaid Cymru
% of votes:	23.9	49.9	15.5	10.8
No. of seats:	8	23	2	3

* See footnote p. 64

Many experts say the Conservatives have very little hold on Wales, and Labour's chief threat is now Plaid Cymru. In the local elections of 1977 Plaid Cymru did better than anyone had expected.

d) Better government is Labour's only •remedy

Ever since the late 19th century the Labour Party grew in importance in Scotland, until it became the dominant party. It was very British in character, especially during the long period of unemployment and general misery in the twenties and thirties. This does not mean that the Labour Party neglected the Scots. It never occurred to them that the Scots were any less British than the English. But now Labour is in serious trouble in Scotland.

Labour's only remedy lies in the quality of government. If, in the next two years, Labour in Scotland is imaginative and progressive in its choice of ministers and policies, it can still take the lead again. If it continues to wait for something to happen, its •supremacy, like that of the Tories, will disappear for ever. And with it may go the United Kingdom.

Christopher Harvie, the New Statesman, Feb. 7th, 1975

Vocabulary

constituency	[kən'stitjuənsi]	district which is represented by an MP at Westminster
laird	[lɛəd]	Scottish word for owner of large estate or property
at ease		natural, feeling at home
constituents	[kən'stitjuənts]	those who have a right to vote in a constituency
remedy	['remidi]	a way to make something/somebody better
supremacy	[sju'preməsi]	being superior to all others; being at the top

2. An Englishman attends an SNP Conference, May 1977

The main subject of the 43rd annual conference of the SNP was independence. The delegates, some 1500 of them, met in a great Victorian meeting hall in Dundee, under a banner that proclaimed, in English and in Gaelic, "Independence – Scotland's Future".

Few people believe here that the SNP is going to win as many as 36 seats at the next general election. The nearer the SNP comes to that magic figure, however, the more unwilling it will be to bother about some •halfway-house assembly. Time is not on the side of the United Kingdom …

Thirty-six seats is the "magic figure" because it would give the SNP a majority of the 71 Scottish seats at Westminster and would give them the right to form a separate Assembly in Scotland (see I. B. 2, p. 16)

To judge from its annual conference the SNP is a real political party, not just a bunch of amateurs. It conducts its business in an orderly but friendly manner. The SNP evidently considers itself to be fun. Policy decisions are taken seriously but not solemnly. Its procedures are somewhat extravagantly democratic and it is absolutily •law-abiding in its approach to the independence struggle. There is a freshness and sense of enthusiasm about the SNP that is to be found nowhere else in the tired •jaundiced state of British politics.
Being nice, however, is not usually enough in politics …

Peter Jenkins believes that the SNP is beginning to attract supporters, not only because it represents the struggle for Scottish independence, but also because of its fresh and enthusiastic approach to politics generally. But he has one fear:

Nonetheless there remains a disturbing quality of innocence in which they approach Scotland's future. Thirty-six seats at Westminster; a negotiation between friends; an independent Scotland. Three easy stages – that in its simplicity is the vision of the future. I hope that the nationalists are correct in believing that if and when the time comes the English will behave as nicely as they intend to behave themselves.

from the Peter Jenkins Column,
the Guardian, May 27th 1977

Vocabulary

halfway-house		half way between no assembly at all, and a proper assembly, i.e. no good for anyone!
law-abiding	[ˈlɔːə.baidiŋ]	obeying the laws of the country
jaundiced	[ˈdʒɔːndist]	jaundice is a disease of the liver. "Jaundiced" is often used to describe feelings of envy, depression, etc.

3. What the industrial bosses think of Devolution

Towards the end of 1977, while Parliament was debating the Devolution Bill, the CBI (Confederation of British Industry) was planning a big campaign against Government proposals for Scottish and Welsh devolution. One •prominent industrialist called devolution a "piece of industrial and economic nonsense". The CBI said they were prepared to go over the heads of the politicians and explain to ordinary Scottish and Welsh people why they shouldn't vote for devolution if there were •referenda.
There was a danger, it was claimed, that devolution might •discourage English-based firms from opening factories in Scotland and Wales. They made it clear that devolution would do nothing for the ordinary Scot and Welshman as regards jobs and security.
The influence of the CBI can be considerable. Industrial financial support helped •pro-marketeers in their EEC referendum campaign.
The CBI has councils in Scotland and Wales which will be organising the campaigns in those countries, with support from the English regions.
On the whole, the industrial bosses support the Conservative Party.

Editor

Vocabulary

prominent	[ˈprɔminənt]	important; well known
referenda	[ˌrefəˈrenda]	pl. of referendum: see p. 6
discourage	[disˈkʌridʒ]	opposite of encourage
pro-marketeers	[prəu-ˈmɑːkitiəz]	those Britons who were in favour of joining the EEC (Common Market)

4. It's fun to be a Scottish Nat these days, but what about the English?

An Englishman examines the causes of Scottish nationalism, and imagines what a free Scotland will be like. He also suggests that England has an unpleasant form of nationalism that few of us are aware of.

(a) Nationalist Scots

From 1945 until the late 1960s, the idea of independence for Scotland was treated as simply comical. Now that small and •lunatic band of separatists has become a threatening army. But why, and why now after 250 years of fairly harmonious union?

The author gives North Sea oil as a reason, but he goes on to suggest a much more interesting cause.

8 Musman, United Kingdom? PB (41035)

I would suggest an answer to the question might be found across the sea in Northern Ireland. The present troubles there started in 1968, a year in which there were explosive crowd politics all over the world – in the United States over Vietnam, in Prague over liberalisation, in Paris over student •grievances, and in London over the need to imitate the Paris students.

The Scottish politicians watched the events in Ulster with great excitement, not to say envy. Scotland had itself long been divided between the Protestants of the eastern Lowlands (see map) and the Catholics, most of them of Irish origin, who •predominate on the Clyde. The battles which used to take place between Celtic and Rangers supporters *(Celtic is a Catholic football team, Rangers are Protestant)*, were almost as •savage as those in Belfast itself.

But now the hatreds are getting less violent all the time, thanks largely to the break-up of the Catholic and Protestant ghettos in Glasgow, and their rehousing in new towns and housing estates. Although the SNP gets more support from the Protestants, many Catholics of Irish origin seem willing to join in a new Scottish nationalism.

Scottish separatist politics, unlike the struggle in Northern Ireland, are painless and fun. Some friends of mine whom I knew in England, and who claim to have a little Scottish blood in them, have found a second youth in the excitement of present-day Edinburgh.

The author goes on to say that Edinburgh is a really exciting place to live in these days compared to "sad, •jaded London". Twice as many English people are emigrating to Australia and even to South Africa than the year before. In Scotland and Wales "separatism", he continues, "is emigration without travelling", and the desire to leave the U.K. is simply the result of disgust with the society created during the past 20 years by the politicians in Westminster.

(b) English nationalism

Why don't the English have a nationalist movement of their own? the letters to newspapers ask. I would suggest that they already do, although it expresses itself in ways that most of us find unpleasant. Anti-Irish and anti-coloured feelings are stronger in England than in other parts of the island, largely because England has received so far all the IRA bomb attacks and most of the two million coloured immigrants. This happened during a period when the English were already depressed by the loss of world reputation, by the poor state of the economy, inflation, no will to work, envy and a general feeling that there was no purpose in anything ...

Scotland with devolution will probably not be very different from Scotland now. Independent Scotland will probably still have ill-managed, strike-bound, old-fashioned factories; the same rotting and filthy skyscraper council blocks; the same new towns smashed and terrorised by the young. Independence for Scotland, Wales and Ulster might leave us with four unhappy and ill-governed pseudo-states instead of one unhappy and ill-governed United Kingdom.

from "Painless Politics in Scotland", by Richard West. The Spectator, August 14, 1976

Vocabulary

lunatic	[ˈluːnətik]	mad, crazy
grievances	[ˈgriːvənsiz]	unpleasant things which have happened to you, and which make you want to complain about them
predominate	[priˈdɔmineit]	here: who form the majority of the population
savage	[ˈsævidʒ]	fierce and wild
jaded	[dʒeidid]	here: looking tired out; the opposite of fresh, lively

D. A Sincere Belief in Devolution – But What about Separatism?

1. Why Devolution is essential.

Extracts from a speech given in Scotland, in March 1976, by Mr Roy Jenkins, at that time a senior minister in the Labour Government:

Successful federal government on American, or German lines was not known in the early 18th century, Mr Jenkins said. "But the fact remains that the loss of the parliament of Scotland (in 1707) has been a cause of real resentment. Matters were made worse in the nineteenth century by the government's lack of interest in Scotland's needs, by the decline in Scotland's industry, by the hundreds of miles separating Scotland from the government in London, and recently and sharply, by the discovery of oil under the North Sea."

Mr Jenkins believed that the real threat to national unity would come if the government was unwilling to offer proper self-government and only went half way, or, worse still, if it raised false hopes.

"This would give narrow nationalists the chance of continuing to create mistrust and discontent among the people. This could indeed lead to the break-up of the United Kingdom."
To achieve a proper balance between the reasonable demands for Scottish control over Scottish affairs, and the equally reasonable needs for democratic and effective United Kingdom government, would require most skilful, strong and sensitive leadership by the government in Parliament.
Mr Jenkins thought the result would depend on four basic principles:
1. the clearest possible definition of the line marking the powers of the devolved assemblies (i.e. a clear line drawn between the responsibilities of the two national assemblies and the responsibilities of the U.K. government at Westminster).
2. the minimum political interference by the Westminster Parliament with Scottish and Welsh institutions.
3. a just and workable method of settling the inevitable conflicts when they arise.

4. the placing of whatever concerns the United Kingdom as a whole under the control of the United Kingdom Parliament.
The fourth principle was essential to preserve the political and economic unity of the United Kingdom, Mr Jenkins said.
The problem was how and where to draw the lines of shared powers (between the Westminster Parliament and the national assemblies) so that the relationship was democratic, efficient and socially just and was therefore likely to be a lasting one.

from a report on Mr Jenkin's speech in
The Times, March 27th 1976

Opinion is divided. Some believe that if an Assembly is granted to the Scots, they will use it to gain complete independence, however limited the powers of the Assembly. Others believe the majority of Scots do not want complete independence, and that an Assembly with reasonable powers will lead them further and further away from separatist ideas. The trouble is, "reasonable" means different things to different people.
As for Wales, the Welsh are not being offered as much self-government as the Scots because no one believes that the majority of Welshman want independence. This cynicism is resented by the Welsh, and many non-Welsh speaking Welsh people now vote Plaid Cymru rather than Labour.

Roy Jenkins

2. A Scottish MP changes his mind.

Mr Robin Cook is a member of Parliament for Edinburgh Central. Here is a résumé of a letter he wrote to Michael Foot, Leader of the House of Commons, in November 1977. Previously, although he was critical of some aspects of Devolution, he had pledged himself to support the Bill.

For the past two years I did feel that most Scots were strongly in favour of devolution. I no longer feel that this is true. In my opinion there is now a lack of interest in devolution in Scotland. I felt this particularly after speaking to a large number of my constituents. They were practically all indifferent to the outcome of the Devolution Bill. Many of them complained that a Scottish Assembly would mean yet another elected body they would be expected to vote for.

I am also disturbed by the powers that Scottish M.P.s would have at Westminster. If the Scots get their Assembly, their M.P.s in the House of Commons would have the right to vote for matters which concern England alone. This, in my opinion, would be completely unjustifiable.

I have supported the Devolution Bill so far, and will continue to do so since I have pledged myself to back the Government. But as soon as the Bill has passed through Parliament, I will consider myself free to campaign against the referendum which will follow.

Robin F. Cook

There are plenty of Scots who would say that Mr Cook is deluding himself and that the SNP feels more confident than ever. No one will know until the next election just how strong are the feelings of the Scots about (1) devolution, (2) independence or separatism. It is impossible to say what effect devolution will have on the U.K. The Liberal Party claims that the Scots must be given a very wide measure of self-government. At the other extreme, many Conservatives believe that would mean the end of the Union. They do not like the idea of a Scottish Assembly, and would give the Scots as little self-government as possible.

In the summer of 1978 it seemed that Mr Cook's views were not mistaken, as is shown by this extract from the New Statesman May 25th 1978:

The SNP are at their lowest ebb for several years but as their publicity vice-chairman pointed out, "When we last had a setback in 1971, the baseline of our support was 15%. Now, it seems to be about 30%. That's not a bad starting-point once optimism has •evaporated about the way the economy is going."

Vocabulary

evaporate [iˈvæpəreit] disappear (slowly)

3. Assemblies for the regions of England?

For some time now it has been suggested that regions like the South West, Yorkshire, East Anglia, should have Assemblies of their own. As Michael Wise writes in the December 1978 number of the Geographical magazine, "there are deep-seated feelings of regional belonging in England". •Devonians, the people of •Norfolk, •Lancastrians, and above all Yorkshiremen are very proud of having their roots in these regions. But there seems so far to be very little desire for political independence in the regions of England, except possibly in Cornwall, with its very much •diluted Celtic population. The inhabitants of these regions are all English, and their Parliament is in Westminster, London. The English are more •conscious of being British than either the Scots or the Welsh. "However," writes Michael Wise, "devolution in Scotland and Wales may set an example." Many people feel that there is too much centralisation in Britain. There could be advisory councils in the regions of England, and also in the big cities. This would give local people a greater democratic control over their own affairs.

Editor

Vocabulary

Devonians [deˈvəunjənz] Devonshire is the central county of the South West. Cornwall is to the west of it.

Norfolk	[ˈnɔːfək]	Norfolk is the northernmost county of East Anglia
Lancastrians	[ˌlæŋkæsˈtriənz]	the people of Lancashire, a large, mostly industrial county in the North West. Lancastrians and Yorkshiremen are neighbours and are great rivals
diluted	[daiˈljuːtid]	made weaker or thinner by the addition of other things. Many people from other parts of the British Isles have settled in Cornwall, and intermarried with the Cornish.
conscious	[ˈkɔnʃəs]	here: aware of having deep-seated feelings about

Exercises

A. Things as they are (or were) before Devolution

1. How much self-rule have Scotland, Northern Ireland and Wales got now (1979)? p. 105
   1. Sum up, in a few words, the differences between Scotland, Northern Ireland and Wales.

B. The Part played by the Different Political Parties in the Devolution Debate

1. Those for and those against the Devolution Bill p. 106
   1. Make a list of those who were against the Devolution Bill and give the reasons why.
   2. What are the attitudes of politicians which worry and even disgust some Welshmen, Scots and Englishmen?
   3. Why did the Government fail to get the Devolution Bill through Parliament in February 1977?

2. Why the Government did not fall – the part played by the Liberals p. 107
   1. The Liberal Party had only 13 MPs after the October 1974 election. Yet after the Government's failure with the Devolution Bill in February 1977, this little group of Liberals played a vital role in keeping the Government in power. What did they offer to do, and what did they demand in return?

3. The Government passes the Devolution Bills p. 108
   1. Do you think the Scots and the Welsh have been given enough self-government in the Devolution Bills?
   2. What would your attitude be if you were English?
   3. In what way will the Scottish Assembly have more power than the Welsh Assembly?

C. The Political Parties in Scotland and Wales

1. Conservatives and Labour p. 109
   1. Analyse the position of the three major parties in Scotland – Labour, Conservative, SNP. Which Party has the least worries? Why is Labour so anxious for the Tories to do well in Scotland? What is the chief worry for both Parties? Consider these questions in making your analysis.

   2. Why do you think the Tories have had decreasing success in General Elections in Scotland?
   3. Study the statistics for the General Election of October 1974 (p. 110). Does anything strike you as strange, or even slightly undemocratic?

2. Better government is Labour's only remedy p. 110
   1. Why is Labour's situation so serious in Scotland, and what has been the cause of it? What might happen if there is no improvement?

3. An Englishman attends an SNP Conference, May 1977 p. 111
   1. List the reasons why Peter Jenkins is impressed by the SNP's performance. How does he compare it with the way British politics are run?
   2. In his article Peter Jenkins has two doubts, one about the SNP, the other about England. What are they?

4. What the industrial bosses think p. 112
   1. What is the meaning of the following phrases:
      1. planning a big campaign
      2. a "piece of industrial and economic nonsense"
      3. they were prepared to go over the heads of the politicians
      4. English-based factories

5. It's fun to be a Scottish Nat these days p. 112
   1. What was happening in 1968 in other parts of the world? What about events in your country at that time? Were they serious?
   2. In the author's opinion, what was one of the chief influences on the SNP?
   3. What has Richard West to say about the English, comparing them to the Scots?
      1. The English have their own form of nationalism. What is it? What excuses does Richard West find for the English?
      2. Does Richard West paint a rosy picture of England if Devolution comes?
      3. Why are separatist politics fun in Scotland? What comparisons does Richard West make?

D. A Sincere Belief in Devolution – but What About Separatism?

1. Why Devolution is essential p. 115
   1. What, in the opinion of Mr Roy Jenkins, might lead to the break-up of the United Kingdom?
   2. What balance is required in settling the problems of Devolution?
   3. Show quite clearly, in your own words, that you understand Mr Jenkin's four basic principles.

2. A Scottish MP changes his mind p. 117
   1. What particularly disturbs Mr Cook about separate Assemblies for Scotland and Wales. Do you think he is justified?

VI. If Devolution Comes – a Fantasy

Suppose that after Devolution Scotland became so •prosperous from her oil that there was a rush of English immigrants – so many that in the end the population of Scotland swelled from 5 million to 45 million and the population of England shrank from 45 million to 5 million. There would be a new balance of power within the United Kingdom.
Here is a satirical fantasy of what might happen ...

"Typically sneaky of the Scots . . . disband their armed forces . . . make the place a tax-haven and leave us to defend their border for them . . ."

The heroes of this fantasy are:

Margaret Ewing,	at present a powerful SNP member of the Westminster Parliament and Vice-President of the SNP
Clement Freud,	an Englishman, one of the 13 Liberal MPs at Westminster. He is also a journalist and broadcaster whose special subject is food. He has advertised dogfood on Commercial TV
Dick Taverne,	an Englishman, once a Labour MP and then an Independent MP
Sir Hugh Fraser,	a wealthy Scottish businessman with business interests in England and Scotland.

It has been officially stated that North Sea oil should make Britain self-sufficient in oil supplies by 1980. What has not been stated is that about the same time several other consequences of the present oil rush will start to make themselves felt.

The Prime Minister gazed through the windows of the Cabinet Room towards Edinburgh Castle. The safest place in the country, she thought to herself with some envy. No car bombs inside there. She looked forward to visiting the Queen there later in the day. She had got into the habit of giving Her Majesty a personal report twice a week on developments in the struggle to crush the English Republican Army (ERA).

"Mistress Ewing," the stage-Glasgow accent of the Minister of Food broke into her momentary dream. "Mistress Ewing, •dinna fash yoursel' but I still say it's no use •greetin' over last night's vote. We could call a general election and get a mandate to destroy the Sassenachs once and for all."

She had been thinking the same thing herself, but the man's manner irritated her. She never knew how serious he was. Besides he would keep putting on that terrible accent.

"Mr Freud," she said, "in the years since you settled here and joined the Scottish National Party you have proved your loyalty. No one questions your loyalty to the party or the nation, any more than they used to question your devotion to that dogfood – Tartan, wasn't it? – you used to advertise. Would you do me the kindness, therefore, and stop trying to sound like a Rangers supporter on a Saturday night."

"Sorry," the Minister of Food said, •reverting to his native southern accent. "Anyway, that's my opinion."

"Thank you. That leaves only the Foreign Secretary, I think, whose view we have not yet heard. Mr Taverne, what do you say?"

"MacTaverne, if you don't mind, Mrs Ewing. Have you forgotten that I changed my name officially yesterday?"

She sighed. It was a sigh of regret for the old days when a Scot was a Scot. Nowadays the party was full of these English immigrants, each one protesting more loudly than the next what a good Scottish patriot he had become. But it was impossible to do without them, the party simply did not have enough native-born politicians and administrators to run a Scotland with its population swollen to 45 million, let alone the whole of the UK.

In some parts of Scotland almost everyone you saw was an immigrant. In Greater Aberdeen, now the industrial and commercial centre of the country, the original inhabitants had become a drop in the ocean of the 10 million who lived there. She remembered how, touring the vast petrochemical complexes, she had heard nothing but cockney voices. Thank goodness the children all spoke like real Aberdonians.

And there was much to be thankful for. The immigrants could so easily have anglicised Scotland, importing not only their possessions and their capital but their political sympathies as well. It had not happened that way. After Scotland had been granted its own Parliament, each wave of new immigrants had •adapted to the environment in which it had found itself. The SNP having become the dominant party at local and provincial government level, the immigrants had •flocked to join the party and declare themselves true, if new, Scots. The change had received the blessing of the Queen when she decided to take up permanent residence in Edinburgh and proclaimed the Scottish Parliament, which now after all represented the great majority of the people of the United Kingdom, to be her principle Parliament. Westminster was now just a provincial Parliament with restricted powers similar to those of Stormont in the days before Ulster had become completely independent.

Even those powers now extended only as far as the Welsh border (for Cardiff enjoyed the same measure of authority as London) and the Scottish border which now ran south of Newcastle. Westminster, at the centre of an area which, apart from tourist reserves, was largely being ploughed up for farmland, had become a •haunt of old men. The Conservative and Labour Parties shared what powers there were, but as far as the English troubles were concerned they had become unimportant.

It was the wild men of the ERA who were causing all the trouble with their demands for complete independence from Scotland. The bombings had started a year ago, with police stations in England as their first •targets. Lately the ERA had •launched a terror campaign, with car bombs causing •havoc in the UK's principal cities – Aberdeen, Inverness, Glasgow, Edinburgh.

The cause of English independence had now been taken up by the official Opposition in Edinburgh, the Scottish Democratic Party. Together with the English MPs in the Edinburgh Parliament, all of whom were since the last general election members of Albion, the political wing of the ERA, the SDP had failed by only one vote to get the house to agree that Scottish troops should be withdrawn from England.

MacTaverne seemed undecided. "I agree that any attack on our Kingdom is most regrettable. But I must warn you that our partners in Europe take a very sympathetic attitude to the English resistance fighters ..."

"Terrorists," interjected the Chancellor of the Exchequer, Sir Hugh Fraser.

"Er yes, I meant terrorists. I think we have to be very careful. My own preference would be to try to solve the problem by a meeting between all members of the UK."

"Nonsense," said Sir Hugh. "You know as well as the rest of us that the English are sitting on the world's biggest unexploited copper deposits in •Lambeth. They can't be allowed to keep that for themselves."

"The Chancellor is right," ruled the Prime Minister. "We shall go to the people and hold an election with that message. I shall ask the Queen for a dissolution of Parliament today. And may God help us all."

by Chad Babble, the Spectator,
January 1st, 1974

Vocabulary

prosperous	[ˈprɔspərəs]	rich, making a lot of money
dinna fash yoursel'		don't worry (Scots)
greetin'		crying, weeping (Scots)
nicht		night (Scots pronunciation)
reverting	[riˈvəːtiˑ]	going back to
adapted to	[əˈdæptid]	changed the way they lived to suit; got used to
flocked	[flɔkt]	large numbers of immigrants had hurried to join
haunt	[hɔːnt]	place where people (or animals) meet or live
target	[ˈtɑːgit]	object or person that you aim at with a bomb or gun
launched	[lɔːntʃt]	here: started
havoc	[ˈhævək]	great destruction
Lambeth	[ˈlæmbəθ]	part of London south of the River Thames
Sassenachs	[ˈsæsənæks]	see p. 26

Exercises and Points of Discussion

1. 1. Mrs Ewing is Prime Minister of what country?
   2. Where do the trouble-makers come from, and what do they call themselves?
   3. What annoys Mrs Ewing about Mr Freud? What is his nationality?
   4. Who is the Foreign Secretary? Why does he call himself *Mac*Taverne?
   5. Why does Mrs Ewing sigh?
   6. How big had the population of the country become as a result of the oil rush?
   7. Which city had become the largest in Scotland, and how large was it?
   8. Which people adapted to the other – the Scots to the English immigrants, or the immigrants to the Scots?
   9. Why did the Queen change her permanent residence to Edinburgh?
   10. What had become of the Parliament at Westminster?
   11. What did the ERA demand, and what do the initials stand for?
   12. The ERA had a lot of sympathisers, both inside and outside Scotland. Why?
   13. What have the English got that they must not be allowed to keep?
2. How far is this piece a satire?
3. Do you find the piece humorous? If so, which passages amuse you most? If not, why not?

Postscript

The Referendum, March 1st 1979

"Yes!" – we want an Assembly. "No!" – we don't.

The results of the Referendum astonished everyone throughout the United Kingdom. One in four Welshmen, and every single region of Wales, voted against an Assembly. Even in the regions where Plaid Cymru are strong, the majority said "No!". One explanation of this massive rejection is the fact that Welsh nationalism is largely cultural and linguistic. Less than 25% of Welshmen speak Welsh today. It is possible that most people in Wales do not feel the need for an Assembly of any sort, but in any case the Assembly offered them by the Bill gave them no real control over their own affairs at all.

In Scotland there were more "Yes" votes than "No" votes. But the "Yes" party did not get anywhere near the 40% of the electorate required. Here are the figures: 62.9% of the electorate voted. Of these, 51.6% said "Yes", while 48% voted "No" (0.4% of the voting papers were spoiled). But here are the figures for the electorate as a whole:

Yes	*No*	*did not vote*
32.5	30.4	37.1

The "No" party claimed that there would have been many more "No"s if the "Yes" party had not put through people's letter-boxes, just before the Referendum, a pamphlet which stated that abstaining (not voting) was as good as voting "No".

Many people believe that a large proportion of Scots did not vote against *an* Assembly, but against *the* Assembly proposed by the Government, which hardly improved the control they already had. The SNP demanded that Scotland must now have an Assemlby, because more people voted "Yes" than "No". The Conservatives and rebel Labour MPs said there could not possibly be a Scottish Assembly when those who voted "Yes" represented less than 33% of the electorate. The decision was left in the hands of the Government and Parliament.

There are those who strongly believe that the future of the United Kingdom lies in federalism, including, as well as Scotland, Wales and Nothern Ireland, the different regions of England.

SHETLAND ISLANDS
ORKNEY ISLANDS
ATLANTIC OCEAN
THE HEBRIDES
LEWIS
NORTH UIST
SOUTH UIST
SKYE
Sea of the Hebrides
SCOTTISH HIGHLANDS
Moray Firth
Loch Ness
Aberdeen
THE GRAMPIANS
SCOTLAND
NORTH SEA
Loch Lomond
Firth of Forth
Glasgow
Edinburgh
Firth of Clyde
NORTHERN IRELAND
Lough Neagh
Belfast
Newcastle upon Tyne
GREAT BRITAIN
PENNINES
ISLE OF MAN
LAKE DISTRICT
ACHILL I.
IRISH SEA
York
Hull
Leeds
ISLE OF ANGLESEY
Dublin
Liverpool
Manchester
ARAN ISLANDS
Sheffield
IRELAND
ENGLAND
The Wash
Cardigan Bay
MTS.
CAMBRIAN
WALES
Birmingham
Coventry
Ouse R.
Norwich
St. George's Channel
Severn R.
Cardiff
Bristol
Thames R.
London
Bristol Channel
Strait of Dover
Southampton
Portsmouth
ISLE OF WIGHT
Plymouth
ENGLISH CHANNEL
SCILLY IS.
ATLANTIC OCEAN
CHANNEL ISLANDS

List for Further Reading

Source material

The Great Hunger (Ireland)	C. Woodham Smith, New English Library
Culloden (Scotland)	J. Prebble, Penguin
The Highland Clearances (Scotland)	J. Prebble, Penguin
Divided Ulster	Liam de Paor, Pelican
Ulster	Sunday Times Insight Team, Penguin
Britain Today (general and non-academic)	Richard Musman, Longman
English Saga	Arthur Bryant, Collins
English Social History	G. M. Trevelyan, Longman and Pelican

Various newspapers and journals:
The Times, Sunday Times, Guardian, New Statesman, Spectator, Listener, Punch, Political Quarterly, Radio Times, The Observer, SNP and Plaid Cymru literature.

Other books

Devolution: the end of Britain?	Tom Dalywell, Jonathan Cape
History of Scotland	R. Michison, UP (paperback)
History of Modern Wales	David Williams, John Murray
History of England	E. L. Woodford, UP paperback)

Fiction

Scotland:
Novels of Sir Walter Scott (1771–1832)
James Bridie – Plays (1888–1951)
Eric Linklater – his novels, but shows his Scottish sympathies especially in his biography of Mary queen of Scots (1894–1974)
James Barrie – Plays, especially "What Every Woman Knows" (1860–1937)
Compton Mackenzie – novels (1883–1972) He was an ardent Scottish Nationalist

Ireland:
Bernard Shaw – "John Bull's Other Island" (play) (1856–1950)
William Yeats – Poetry (1865–1939)
Sean O'Casey – Plays: "Shadow of a Gunman"
"Juno and the Paycock"
"The Plough and the Stars"
written (1923–1926)
Liam O'Flaherty – his novels: "The Informer" (1925)
"Black Soul" (1924)
"Insurrection" (1950). It is about the Easter Rising, 1916.
J. M. Synge – Plays: "Riders to the Sea" (1907)
"Playboy of the Western World" (1904)

Brendan Behan – Plays: "Quare Fellow" (1957)
"The Hostage" (1959)

(Brendan Behan led a stormy, revolutionary life and fought for a while with the IRA. He also spent 6 years in a Dublin jail for wounding a policeman).

Wales:

Kate Roberts – her novels. She wrote in Welsh but the following novels were translated:
"Summer Day" (1946)
"From the Swamp of the Hills" (1925)
"Gossip Street" (1949)

Richard Llewellyn – his novels:
"How Green was my Valley" (1939). It is about Welsh miners.
"None but the Lonely Heart" (1943)